Trade Issues in the Mid 1980s

by Sidney Golt

and

A Policy Statement

by the
British-North American Committee

BRITISH-NORTH AMERICAN COMMITTEE

Sponsored by
British-North American Research Association (U.K.)
National Planning Association (U.S.A.)
C.D. Howe Institute (Canada)

ISBN 0-902594-42-7

Published by the British-North American Committee

Printed and bound in the United Kingdom by
Contemprint Limited, London SE1

October 1982

Contents

The British-North American Committee..................INSIDE FRONT COVER

"Anyone for Tennis?" vii

**A POLICY STATEMENT ON TRADE ISSUES IN THE MID 1980s
by the British-North American Committee**............................ ix

Members of the Committee Signing the Statement............................. xiii

Author's Preface... xvii

**TRADE ISSUES IN THE MID 1980s
by Sidney Golt**

I The Background 1

II The Tokyo Round Agreements, 1979 5
   THE TARIFF AGREEMENT.. 5
   THE NON-TARIFF PACKAGE.. 6
     Technical Agreements 7
     • Customs Valuation 7
     • Technical Barriers to Trade............................. 7
     • Import Licensing Procedures............................. 7
     Agriculture 8
     Framework for the Conduct of International Trade........... 8
     • Developing Countries 8
     • Notification, Consultation, Dispute Settlement and
      Surveillance 9
     • Safeguard Measures...................................... 9
     Civil Aircraft... 10
     Major Codes 10
     • Government Procurement.................................. 10
     • Subsidies and Countervailing Duties.................... 11

III Trade Policy Developments, 1980-1982 13
   GOVERNMENT DECLARATIONS....................................... 13
   DAY-TO-DAY WORK... 14
     Tariff Issues.. 15
     • Effective Tariff Levels................................. 15
     • Harmonisation of Nomenclature 15
     • Negotiation about Particular Items 16

The Non-Tariff Agreements 16
- Meaning of Accession to the Codes 16
- Customs Valuation Code................................. 17
- Standards Code 17
- Import Licensing Procedures............................ 17
- Agricultural Arrangements 20
- Civil Aircraft.. 20
- Code on Government Procurement 20
- Developing Countries 20
- Safeguards 20
- Subsidies Code 20
GOVERNMENT ACTIONS AND
INTERNATIONAL RELATIONS............................. 21

IV National Stances and International Conflicts, 1982.................. 27
THE UNITED STATES AND THE
EUROPEAN COMMUNITY................................. 28
The US View... 28
- Agriculture.. 29
- Steel.. 30
The Community View 30
- Agriculture.. 31
- Steel.. 32
- US Recourse to the GATT.............................. 32
THE US/EUROPEAN COMMUNITY AND JAPAN 32
The Community View 33
The US View... 35

THE UNITED STATES AND CANADA 37
THE INDUSTRIALISED/DEVELOPING COUNTRIES 39

V The GATT Ministerial Meeting: November 1982...................... 43
PERCEPTIONS OF PURPOSE................................. 43
THE WORK OF THE MEETING 45
The Declaration.. 46
Matters for "Decision" 47
- Developing Countries 47
- Safeguards 49
- Agriculture.. 50
- General Tariff and Non-Tariff Measures........................... 51
- Disputes Settlement 51

Matters for Future Examination, and Possible Future
Extensions of the GATT... 53
• Services... 53
• Trade-Related Investment Issues....................................... 54
• Trade in High Technology Products................................... 54

VI **Conclusion**... 57

Appendices
I Address by Mr. Arthur Dunkel, Director-General, General
Agreement on Tariffs and Trade, at "Ostasiatisches Liebesmahl",
Hamburg, 5th March 1982.. 59
II European Commission Communication to the Council: General
Policy Orientation for the GATT Ministerial Meeting
(November 1982).. 65
III An Extract from Representations to the Japanese Government
by the European Community Pursuant to Article XXIII,
Paragraph 1 of the GATT, April 7th 1982................................ 72
IV US Position in the International Trading Arena. A review by
US Special Trade Representative William Brock, before a Trade
Subcommittee of the House of Representatives, October 28th
1981 and before the House Ways and Means Committee
October 29th 1981.. 75

Members of the British-North American Committee............................ 87

Sponsoring Organisations... 92

Publications of the British-North American Committee....................... 94

ANYONE FOR TENNIS?

In the good old days we played,
Like decent chaps, the game of trade,
So, what the umpire said was that,
 According to the rules of GATT,
Was taken, in the name of sport,
As ruling sanctions out of court;
And no ungentlemanly shout
 Disputed when the ball was out.

But now, alas, the urge to win,
Has brought a breach of discipline;
With all the seeded players free
 To denigrate the referee.
And go for game, and set, and match
By any rules their leaders hatch
Which give their overseas accounts
 The better of the trading bounce.

For all the players it is vital
That no one else should win the title,
Though, what they can themselves produce,
 May get them, at the best, to deuce;
So beggaring my neighbour's trade
Is how the winning lobs are made,
While players, point-by-point, dispute
 Who brought the game to disrepute.

Americans, for whom it's sin
To play the game unless they win,
Are most inclined to hedge their bet
 By doubling up the height of net;
This stops the European ball
From entering their court at all,
While Europe threatens to retire,
 Or raise its own a sanction higher.

But both accuse the Eastern set
Of dirty play around the net,
And call the Japanese a menace
 Unworthy of the game of tennis;
Or fight about the repercussions
Of playing doubles with the Russians,
In case the Eastern Bloc attack its
 Service game with Western rackets.

The players, to a man, deplore
The ones who call the game a war;
Insisting it is only played,
 Within the spirit of free trade,
By gentlemen who don't resort
To cheating in the name of sport;
It's simply not the game for fools
 Who keep insisting on the rules!

Bertie Ramsbottom

Reproduced by Courtesy of the Editor of the *Financial Times* and the author, Ralph Windle.

A Policy Statement on Trade Issues in the Mid-1980s by the British-North American Committee

We are pleased to issue this third in a series of publications on multilateral trade by the distinguished British authority, Sidney Golt. While his two previous monographs* reported on progress in implementing the basic commitments agreed to in Tokyo in 1973, Mr Golt now discusses world trade issues that are currently emerging and which the GATT Ministers will consider at Geneva in November 1982 with a view to further common action.

This publication appears at a most critical time. The world's trading nations now face a daunting constellation of circumstances, both long and short term, that challenge their post-war achievement of creating a more open trading system.

- They are experiencing just now the most serious recession and highest level of unemployment since the present liberal trade movement began almost 40 years ago.

- In these circumstances, the very progress of previous negotiating rounds towards developing a world marketplace is now beeing seen by some countries, or particular economic sections within them, as threatening their prosperity rather than offering new opportunities.

- Quite apart from the impact of current recession, concern has been growing in several leading industrial countries over a gradual decline in their traditional competitive prowess.

- Meanwhile, international competition is often influenced perversely by exchange rate shifts reacting to monetary policies rather than to trade performance.[1]

- Responding to the consequences of these factors—unemployment in particular—many nations have resorted to overt or covert protectionist measures. Often these are associated with bilateral confrontations

---

*Sidney Golt: *The GATT Negotiations, 1973-1975; A Guide to the Issues (1974)* and *The GATT Negotiations 1973-1979: the Closing Stage (1978)*. British-North American Committee, London, Washington and Montreal.

1   *While reference is made to the impact of exchange rates on trade distortions, I believe that this is a point that should be given more consideration in international fora such as the IMF and possibly in GATT.*

Since the introduction of floating exchange rates there have been varying degrees of intervention by Governments in the market. As a result, there are temptations which should be resisted and perhaps identified with a view to ensuring that trading nations foreswear with very clear rules further distortions of trade conditions brought about by changes in the exchange rate which result in ranges differing from that which would be achieved in a free market situation—**Ian MacGregor**

among the three major trading entities (the United States, the European Community and Japan) and between the United States and Canada the single largest trading partnership.

● An additional response has emerged—what Mr. Golt calls "perhaps the most important new dimension in thinking about international commercial policy in many years". This is a shift in national industrial policies from measures that are genuine attempts to adjust to new competition, to those which are simply new methods of protection designed to save jobs at all costs.

This escalation of challenges and responses is sowing doubts about the desirability of maintaining the open world trading system. These doubts are only encouraged by the striking contrast between the allegiance which governments pledge to its preservation through habitual statements of their Ministers at international meetings and the policies which they tolerate and even promote at home.

In our view, the choice is not between mere ritualistic reiteration of the general virtues of open trade on the one hand and its wholesale abandonment on the other. Instead, we must find ways to bridge the widening gap in our perceptions of the world trading system between one that is economically sound over the long run and one that is politically achievable in democratic societies at this critical time.

In the last analysis, the key is to devise appropriate methods of adjustment to increasing competition. By this we mean those approaches that encourage firms to enhance their own competitiveness rather than compensate for its deficiencies, or, in cases where the potential for this process does not exist, policies that will encourage the shift of resources no longer economic to new activities. Here the record within our countries shows some promising examples of adaptation, notably where a significant measure of co-operation between management and trade unions has been evident. The US textile industry, considered doomed fifteen years ago, now exports more than it imports. Unprecedented efforts are now being undertaken to reorganise the production of steel in the United Kingdom and automobiles in the United States.

Still, we must recognise the threats of serious and often irreversible disruption which now overhang many of the large employment industries in virtually all countries, threats that can overpower even the most dedicated efforts toward adjustment. Thus it is unrealistic at this time to expect such industries, their associated labour forces, and their respective governments to acquiesce in sharp and serious curtailment of production, especially when this appears likely to be permanent.

We therefore accept that in the present situation of world recession, governments will occasionally deem it necessary to prevent social disruption and heavy unemployment by taking measures that are contrary to the general principles of open trading and adaptation to changing world economic circumstances. We do however regard it as of the utmost importance than when such measures are taken they do the least possible injury to the interests of other participants in the open trading system, and are not maintained longer than is essential. We also believe that the eventual damage that such measures impose upon the economies of nations taking them should be fully and openly recognised. [2&3]

All this means that those who are concerned with the future of the world trading system—and this certainly includes the members of the British-North American Committee—must now expand the areas of their traditional thinking on the subject. To be sure, we must honour the commitments made during the Tokyo Round, address the important business left unfinished, and consider extending the GATT rules and processes to new areas—in short, we should follow the agenda outlined by Mr. Golt in his fifth chapter. But, beyond all this, we must undertake a challenging new task: to re-assess the world trading system and explore new ways of adjusting to present realities without retreating from fundamental commitments to keeping it truly open.

In our opinion, this difficult, delicate and evolutionary task should begin as part of the agenda for the GATT Ministers this November. But we also believe that this reappraisal should engage the private sectors in our three countries as well, especially those who lead businesses and organised labour—the persons whose decisions most directly affect production and employment.

The British-North American Committee awaits with keen interest the readiness of the GATT Ministers to accept this challenge. And, for its part, our diverse membership will join in the search for appropriate responses to it.

---

2 *I concur generally with the sentiments expressed in the footnote by Hendrik Houthakker, Donald Jacobs and Charles Wootton. Protectionism in its current manifestations is essentially a retreat from reality.*

If protective measures have to be resorted to, for whatever reason, it is imperative that they should not be such as to remove from the industries affected the pressure to adapt to current and expected future world trading conditions.

*It is also essential that the general economic management of the country applying such measures should be such as to encourage the process of adaptation and the development of new forms of productive employment. Otherwise, people displaced from industries that need to adapt will not be reabsorbed, opportunities for newcomers to the employment market will be reduced, and the economy will not prosper in an inevitably ever more interdependent trading world—*Sir Richard Powell

3 *I do not take it as an article of faith that government intervention to prevent severe disruption of key industries by import surges necessarily causes damage to the domestic economy in the long run. Eventual outcome depends on the effectiveness of policies to ease adjustment and structural changes—*George J. Poulin

FOOTNOTES TO THE STATEMENT AS A WHOLE

*Subsidisation is leading to unilateral counter-actions which could undermine much of the progress in reducing tariffs that has been made under GATT. The case of one or more governments subsidising a given industry to engage in a price war with another country is politically unacceptable in the afflicted country. The trend towards state-owned industries that are prepared to accept losses in export trade exacerbates the problem. Proof of injury is so time-consuming that an entire industry can be put in jeopardy before effective action can be taken within the framework of GATT. The only solution may be to withdraw the proof of injury provision and return to mandatory imposition of countervailing duties in the case where direct operating subsidises can be proven—***Gerald Heffernan***

We must disassociate ourselves emphatically from the encouragement, qualified though it is, to protectionism in the covering statement. One of the developments that aggravated the downturn of 1929-1930 into the great depression was the adoption of the Hawley-Smoot Tariff by the US followed by international measures elsewhere. The resulting disintergration of the international trade took decades to correct.

In the present circumstances the dangers of protectionism are even greater. The world economy has become more integrated and most large firms are now international in scope. The liberalisation in trade during the sixties and seventies has been a positive factor for consumers, workers and managers in all countries. Assistance for those adversely impacted to help them adapt to changing circumstances may sometimes be needed, but protectionism is not the answer. All too often, protection merely serves to preserve a status quo that has become obsolete.

*Instead of condoning a return to the thirties, BNAC should reaffirm its commitment to a free and open international order. This is not only good economics but the frictions inevitable under the spreading protectionism would also have serious political repercussions. The present troubles in the world economy are not due to trade liberalisation and it would be short-sighted to export domestic problems to other countries—***Hendrik S. Houthakker, Donald P. Jacobs and Charles G. Wootton***

Mr. Golt focusses primarily on the current trade relationships of the developed countries. Since I represent workers in labour intensive industries, the trade relationships between these countries and the LDC's have greater importance for me. Given the fact that LDC markets are the most closed, that their exports are generally the most subsidised and that they apply the greatest "performance requirements" on investment—while on the other hand American unemployment is at intolerable levels—the current upcoming GATT Ministerial meeting agenda is inadequate in addressing this important problem area.

Over the last few years, the LDC's have been overwhelmingly concerned with the great drop in commodity and raw material prices, rather than MTN tariff and Tokyo Round code issues. Only lately have they focused on the Ministerial Meeting and they are still in the process of formulating their position and demands for the meeting.

*Once the LDC stance has been formulated and demands put on the table, I, Mr. Golt and the full BNAC Committee can respond in more adequate fashion to what will be the trade issues of the mid-80's—***Jacob Sheinkman***

Members of the Committee Signing the Statement

RICHARD W. FOXEN
Corporate Vice President—International,
Rockwell International Corp.

SIR ALISTAIR FRAME
Deputy Chairman and Chief Executive,
Rio-Tinto Zinc Corporation

THEODORE GEIGER
Distinguished Research Professor of
Intersocietal Relations,
School of Foreign Service,
Georgetown University

MALCOLM GLENN
Executive Vice President,
Reed Holdings Incorporated

GEORGE GOYDER
Sudbury, Suffolk

JOHN H. HALE
Senior Vice President,
Alcan Aluminum Limited

HON. HENRY HANKEY
British Secretary,
BNAC, Westerham, Kent

FRED L. HARTLEY
Chairman and President,
Union Oil Company of California

*G. R. HEFFERNAN
President,
Co-Steel International Limited

ROBERT HENDERSON
Chairman,
Kleinwort Benson Limited

SIR TREVOR HOLDSWORTH
Chairman,
Guest, Keen & Nettlefolds Limited

*HENDRIK S. HOUTHAKKER
Professor of Economics,
Harvard University

*DONALD P. JACOBS
Dean,
J. L. Kellog Graduate School of
Management, Northwestern University

JOHN V. JAMES
Chairman of the Board and
Chief Executive Officer,
Dresser Industries, Inc.

JOSEPH D. KEENAN
President,
Union Label and Service Trades
Department, AFL-CIO

C. CALVERT KNUDSEN
Chairman and Chief Executive Officer,
MacMillan Bloedel Limited

H. U. A. LAMBERT
Chairman,
Barclays Bank International Limited

FRANKLIN A. LINDSAY
Chairman, Executive Committee,
Itek Corporation

SIR PETER MACADAM
Chairman,
B.A.T. Industies Ltd.

IAN MacGREGOR
Honorary Chairman,
AMAX Inc.

J. P. MANN
Deputy Chairman,
United Biscuits (Holdings) Limited

A. B. MARSHALL
Chairman,
Bestobell Limited

DONALD K. McIVOR
Chairman and Chief Executive Officer,
Imperial Oil Limited

DONALD E. MEADS
Chairman and President,
Carver Associates,

SIR PATRICK MEANEY
Group Managing Director,
Thomas Tilling Limited

SIR PETER MENZIES
Welwyn, Hertfordshire

JOHN MILLER
Vice Chairman,
National Planning Association

ALLEN E. MURRAY
President of Marketing and Refining
Division,
Mobil Oil Corporation

KENNETH D. NADEN
President,
National Council of Farmer Cooperatives

WILLIAM S. OGDEN
Vice Chairman and
Chief Financial Officer,
The Chase Manhattan Bank, N.A.

BROUGHTON PIPKIN
Stow-on-the-Wold, Gloucestershire

See footnote to the Statement.

*GEORGE J. POULIN
General Vice President,
International Association of Machinists &
Aerospace Workers

*SIR RICHARD POWELL
Hill Samuel Group Limited

ALFRED POWIS
Chairman,
Noranda Mines Limited

PAUL E. PRICE
Executive Vice President,
Direct-to-Consumer,
Businesses and Chemicals,
Quaker Oats Company

LOUIS PUTZE
Ligonier, Pennsylvania

BEN ROBERTS
Professor of Industrial Relations,
London School of Economics

HAROLD B. ROSE
Group Economic Advisor,
Barclays Bank Limited

CHESTER A. SADLOW
President,
Europe/Africa/Middle East,
Westinghouse Electric Corporation

DAVID SAINSBURY
Director of Finance,
J. Sainsbury Limited

WILLIAM R. SALOMON
Limited Partner and Honorary Member
of the Executive Committee,
Salomon Brothers

A. C. I. SAMUEL
Handcross, Sussex

NATHANIEL SAMUELS
Chairman, Advisory Director,
Lehman Brothers Kuhn Loeb Inc.

LORD SEEBOHM
Dedham, Essex

*JACOB SHEINKMAN
Secretary-Treasurer,
Amalgamated Clothing and Textile
Workers' Union

LORD SHERFIELD
Director,
Badger Limited

R. MICHAEL SHIELDS
Managing Director,
Associated Newspapers Group Limited

GEORGE L. SHINN
Chairman and Chief Executive Officer,
The First Boston Corporation

GORDON R. SIMPSON
Chairman,
General Accident Fire and
Life Assurance Corporation Limited

SIR ROY SISSON
Chairman,
Smiths Industries Limited

SIR LESLIE SMITH
Chairman,
BOC International Limited

RALPH I. STRAUS
New York, N.Y.

SIR ROBERT TAYLOR
Deputy Chairman,
Standard Chartered Bank Limited

JAMES C. THACKRAY
President,
Bell Canada

WILLIAM C. THOMSON
A Managing Director,
Royal Dutch/Shell Group of Companies

ALEXANDER C. TOMLINSON
President,
National Planning Association

ALAN TUFFIN
General Secretary,
Union of Communication Workers

WILLIAM I. M. TURNER, JR.
President and Chief Executive Officer,
Consolidated-Bathurst Inc.

W. O. TWAITS
Toronto, Ontario

WILLIAM L. WEARLY
Chairman, Executive Committee,
Ingersoll-Rand Company

VISCOUNT WEIR
Vice Chairman,
The Weir Group Limited

*CHARLES WOOTTON
Senior Director, Foreign and Domestic,
Policy Analysis and Planning,
Gulf Oil Corporation

See footnote to the Statement.

Author's Preface

In 1973-1974 and again in 1977-1978, the British-North American Committee gave me the opportunity to examine and comment on the matters at issue in the multilateral trade negotiations which were inaugurated by the GATT Ministerial Meeting in Tokyo in September 1973—the "Tokyo Round"—and on the progress of the negotiations. In the two Reports which resulted and which were published by the BNAC in 1974 and 1978, I tried to give a background sketch of the development of international commercial policy in the post-war period, and an analytical account of the substance of the negotiations and of the attitudes and approaches of the main participants in them.

It was part of my aim in those Reports to provide a reasonably continuous record of the events and the issues, and I have been encouraged to believe that they have been of some general value in this respect. I am therefore again most grateful to the British-North American Committee for enabling me to bring the record up to date with this third Report.

The 1978 publication was written a little over a year before the end of the Tokyo Round, and discussed what at that time seemed likely to be the outcome. In this 1982 Report, I have carried the story forward, and have tried

(i) to give a summary and an assessment of the results of the Tokyo Round;

(ii) to describe the developments in commercial policy, both inside the GATT organisation in Geneva and in the attitudes and actions of the main participants in world trade during the three years since the end of the Round; and

(iii) on a broader front, to look at the underlying issues and problems for world trade and international commercial policy on the eve of another GATT Ministerial Meeting to be held in Geneva in November 1982, and to assess the prospects for that meeting.

The opportunity to continue discussion on these topics with friends and former colleagues—in the GATT and other international organisations and both inside and outside government service—and, on this occasion, to make contact with some of a new generation of participants in the forming of policy and the conduct of negotiations, has given me great pleasure as well as much assistance. I am grateful to all of them, in London, Ottawa, Washington, Paris, Brussels and Geneva, for their help and their time.

I have also to thank the BNAC both for their continued interest in the subject and for the discussions on it at their meetings at Palm Beach in 1981 and at Torquay in June 1982. It was particularly agreeable to be associated again—so many years after serving under him when he was Permanent Secretary of the Board of Trade—with Sir Richard Powell. Simon Webley and Melanie Walsh have as always been most patient and generous with their help, and I owe special gratitude to Sperry Lea in Washington for his devoted, meticulous and unfailingly valuable editorial and presentational advice.

As in the previous Reports, my intention is to analyse and inform rather than to make judgements. In presenting the views held in various countries or sectors, I have put these forward as they are argued by the protagonists; this implies neither endorsement nor condemnation of those views. Equally, in so far as views or judgements emerge, they are, of course, entirely my own, and not necessarily those of the BNAC or of any of the people with whom I have had discussions.

It may indeed be in this Report that I have not been able to disguise the fact that the pleasure I have had in preparing it is mixed with considerable sadness about some of the conclusions to which I am driven by my review of the present world situation, and of the conflicts and dangers which now face us. I therefore feel even more strongly than I did when I wrote my Preface to the 1974 Report that the tripartite co-operation between Britain, Canada and the United States which is manifested by the British-North American Committee has a continuing and important contribution to make to the restoration of civilised international relations in commercial policy and of the expansion of world trade.

September 1982   SIDNEY GOLT

SIDNEY GOLT was formerly Advisor on Commercial Policy to the Board of Trade and a Deputy Secretary of the Department of Trade and Industry until 1970. He is now Advisor on International Commercial Policy to the International Chamber of Commerce, and a member of the international consultancy firm, Malmgren, Golt, Kingston and Co., Ltd.

Trade Issues in the Mid 1980s

I The Background

In November 1982, Ministers from all the countries which are members of the General Agreement on Tariffs and Trade (GATT) and of other countries associated with it are due to meet in Geneva to consider the problems which face international trade. The meeting will be the 1982 Annual Session of the GATT Contracting Parties. In most years, countries are represented in the Session by officials, but this year the meeting will take place at Ministerial level, and it will be the first Ministerial meeting of the GATT since the Tokyo meeting in September 1973, which initiated the Tokyo Round of multilateral trade negotiations.

The Tokyo Round was concluded in 1979, at the end of a very troubled decade in world economic affairs and international trade relations.

The years since the end of World War II have followed a convenient habit of falling rather neatly into periods of about ten years, each with its own characteristic trends. Following the working out of the post-war economic settlement in the second half of the 1940's, and the establishment of the Bretton Woods institutions and the GATT, the 1950's were a period of reconstruction and recovery, leading to the restoration of convertability of currencies, and marked, at the end, by the transition from the Organisation for European Economic Co-operation (OEEC) to the Organisation for Economic Co-operation and Development (OECD) and the creation of the European Economic Community and the European Free Trade Association. The 1960's proved to be a decade of consolidation, but also of emerging strains on the system. They saw the negotiation of the Kennedy Round of tariff reductions, the birth of many newly independent countries, and the creation of the United Nations Conference on Trade and Development (UNCTAD), with the beginnings of the intense debate between developed and developing countries; and they closed with the substantial problems in trade and monetary relations between the United States and the rest of the world which culminated in the "Nixon measures" of August 1971. These ended the ability of the rest of the world to rely on the United States to perform a number of stabilising functions in the world economy—as a lender of last resort, and with a currency serving as a base of valuation for all others. The 1970's emerged, for this and other reasons—outstandingly the oil price shocks of 1973 and since—as a period of very great unease in international economic relations.

The problems which had faced the world as the aftermath of the changed relationship between the United States and other countries, and which had led to the ending in August 1971 of dollar convertibility, imposed on the major industrial countries an inescapable duty to try to find some solutions, or at least ameliorations. The Smithsonian Agreement of December, 1971, did not solve the monetary crisis, but it did something to ease it, even if only temporarily. On the trade front, intensive bilateral discussions led eventually to the September, 1973 meeting in Tokyo, and to a commitment from the United States, the European Community and Japan, to undertake full scale trade negotiations. These were to cover not only tariffs, but a wide range of government measures affecting international trade. These Tokyo Round negotiations, as things turned out, lasted from their start in 1973 till virtually the end of the decade. During this period there was a somewhat cautious truce in international trade policy, though with many manifestations of growing pressures for protectionism. Given the difficulties of the period, including especially the persistent world economic depression, it may perhaps be said that the preservation of the processes of international trade without even greater dislocation than did in fact occur provides evidence of the basically sound foundations of the GATT system.

My two previous Reports for the British-North American Committee[1] gave an account of the various stages of the Tokyo Round, and carried the story forward to the spring of 1978, when the negotiations were moving into their decisive period. It is not necessary now to go into the details of the negotiations, but we shall describe in the following sections the final outcome, and the course of events since 1979. At this stage, it is worth restating the final paragraph of "The GATT Negotiations 1973-1979: The Closing Stage":

---

1 Sidney Golt: *The GATT Negotiations, 1973-1975; A Guide to the Issues, (1974)*, and *The GATT Negotiations 1973-1979; The Closing Stage* (1978), British-North American Committee, London, Washington and Montreal.

"It would no doubt be an improvement on the existing situation if the Tokyo Round produced a new and credible re-affirmation of the basic premises of the liberal trading system, even if the price of doing so included some moderate and strictly controlled derogation from the GATT in its present form. The important thing is to maintain sufficient confidence in the basic will of governments to reverse their current drift into economic nationalism. It is less easy to feel such confidence quite so unqualifiedly now than it was even when the Tokyo Round was inaugurated. There is, of course, no lack of protestation by governments on the subject. The test will be furnished by their actions."

The Tokyo Round outcome did in fact represent a very substantial achievement in many respects, even if, as we shall see, there were in some areas, gaps or shortcomings. The machinery was put in place to create the possibility of new birth for an enlarged GATT - a network of Agreements covering a much wider range of government activity than tariffs alone. The declarations of government spokesmen held out the hope that the conclusion of the negotiations could be followed by a new impulse for international co-operation, so as to make the 1980's a period of substantially greater stability and order in international trade relations, and expansion in international trade.

However, in the event, the years since the end of the Tokyo Round have seen increasing turmoil and difficulty for international trade; and it was in the light of this, and especially of the implications for the world trading system of the world-wide slowdown in economic activity, that in June 1981 the Consultative Group of 18 Member countries of the GATT met to discuss the situation. The Consultative Group is an informal high level official group which steers GATT activity, on behalf of the 86 GATT Contracting Parties. The Group noted that some countries had considered it necessary to introduce trade-restrictive measures; and that pressures for bilateral arrangements to regulate exports in certain sensitive sectors had grown. The trade and payments situation of many developing countries continued to give rise to concern and necessitated their fuller participation in world trade. It was important that there should be a strong political commitment on the part of governments to the maintenance and improvement of the multilateral trading system.

The Group concluded that it would be appropriate for a ministerial meeting of GATT Contracting Parties to be held during the second half of 1982, to allow a political analysis of the difficulties confronting international trade in the 1980's.

The final decision to hold such a meeting was taken unanimously at the GATT annual Session on 25th November 1981[2], when it was agreed that the 1982 annual Session should be convened at Ministerial level. The purpose of the meeting was defined as being "to examine the functioning of the multilataral trading system, and to reinforce the common efforts of the contracting parties to support and improve the system for the benefit of all nations." Ministers would address themselves to four topics:

"(i) the implementation of the results of the Multilateral Trade Negotiations;

 (ii) problems affecting the trading system;

(iii) the position of developing countries in world trade; and

(iv) future prospects for the development of trade.

Finally, in the context of their consideration of the work programme of the GATT for the 1980's, Ministers would also determine future priorities for co-oporation among contracting parties."

It is against this background that we have now to turn to examination of the Tokyo Round outcome and subsequent events, including especially—since they are crucial for the whole picture—the policies and actions of the major participants in world trade, the United States, the European Community and Japan.

---

2 *GATT Activities in 1981.* GATT, Geneva, 1982 p.27.

II The Tokyo Round Agreements, 1979

The Tokyo Round negotiations produced a formidable "package" of agreements, on a wide variety of matters. They covered, on the one hand, tariff reductions and, on the other, a substantial series of agreements (often referred to as "codes") and understandings about non-tariff measures. In sheer volume of documents, the outcome was certainly very productive; and many of the topics dealt with were of very great importance.

The list is worth setting out in full under their formal titles:

   (i) Geneva (1979) Protocol & Supplementary Protocol; (these, with their schedules, deal with the tariff reductions agreed and with the arrangements for phasing the reductions)

  (ii) Agreement on Technical Barriers to Trade

 (iii) Agreement on Government Procurement

  (iv) Agreement on Interpretation & Application of Articles VI, XVI and XXIII (this deals with subsidies and countervailing duties)

   (v) Arrangement regarding Bovine Meat

  (vi) International Dairy Arrangement

 (vii) Agreement on Implementation of Article VII; (this deals with Customs Valuation)

(viii) Agreement on Import Licensing Procedures

  (ix) Agreement on Trade in Civil Aircraft

   (x) Agreement on Implementation of Article VI (this deals with anti-dumping)

  (xi) Decisions about Differential and More Favourable Treatment, Reciprocity and Fuller Participation by Developing Countries

 (xii) Safeguards

(xiii) Declaration on Trade Measures taken for Balance-of-Payments Purposes

 (xiv) Understanding Regarding Notification, Consultation, Dispute Settlement and Surveillance.

In the discussion which follows, these have been regrouped for convenience.

THE TARIFF AGREEMENT

The Geneva protocols envisaged reductions in the levels of duty by the major industrial countries, adding up to an average cut of one-third of the existing levels, and to an important degree of convergence or harmonisation in national tariff structures. In addition, many other smaller countries also agreed to reductions in their tariffs. On a total global basis, it was suggested by GATT calculations at the time that the scale of the cuts was only slightly less than those resulting from the Kennedy Round. There were, of course, some sectors with less than average reductions (notably textiles). There was also a sizable list of exceptions, so that even in some of the major countries there remain a few peaks, even though, in general, the particular formula used meant that a number of the US peaks were brought much nearer to the European common external tariff level. However, if the percentage cut of tariff levels is translated to the absolute levels of actual rates, the picture is less dramatic. The average tradeweighted level of the European Community's common external tariff for industrial goods before the end of the Tokyo Round was about 9.8%. At the end of the reduction process, the figure will be about 7.5%. The process was, moreover, scheduled to take place in annual stages over an eight year period running to 1987. The Community's reductions, therefore, run at an average, in actual tariff points, of 0.3% a year.

It also seemed, at the time of the end of the Tokyo Round, that this would be, for a quite considerable time to come, the last substantial step in tariff reduction. From this point of view, there seemed to be a distinct change of mood over the decade of the 1970's. At the beginning of the decade it had been widely taken for granted that there should be a continuing series of mutual tariff reductions, at any rate by the major countries, which would eventually lead to their total elimination. The high level committee, under M. Jean Rey's chairmanship, appointed by the OECD in 1970, recommended that this should be the outcome of a ten year transition period. The 1987 outcome of the Tokyo Round will fall considerably short of it. It still remains extremely unlikely that there will be any general round of tariff negotiations during the 1980's, but there may be negotiations in some areas.

THE NON-TARIFF PACKAGE

Whatever the scale and significance of the Tokyo Round tariff agreement, this was not, and was not claimed to be, the most important element of the package. Far more interest was attached to the agreements or "codes" on non-tariff measures.

Technical Agreements

The first group of these is technical in character—on customs valuation, on technical barriers to trade (more usually described as the barriers resulting from differing national standards specifications) and on import licensing procedures. On each of these some quite significant new ground was broken.

In the Agreement on *Customs Valuation*, the general principle was established that tariffs should be assessed on the "actual value" of the imported goods, not on the values of similar products of national origin or on arbitrary or fictitious values. It was also agreed that the normal way of establishing the value should be the price in the invoice for the transaction; and other rules designed to introduce much greater certainty into valuation procedures were included. This Code thus contained new obligations of real substance, including the ending of the long standing grievance against United States valuation of imports of some chemicals at American prices for assessment of duties.

The Agreement for *Technical Barriers to Trade* was rather more procedural. It did not set out to draw up new technical regulations or standards, or testing and certification schemes, which fall within the activities of other institutions and organisations. But it aimed to encourage the adoption of international standards, and their adoption by governments for domestic regulations, wherever appropriate; to provide a notification procedure designed to keep all signatories informed about standards under preparation, supplemented by the creation of enquiry points to ensure transparency of information; to establish, for the first time, some binding rules of conduct of governments to enable complaints in this area to be brought under an international discipline; and to apply quite specifically the GATT rule of "national treatment"—non-discrimination against foreigners—in technical regulations.

The Agreement on *Import Licensing Procedures* set out various rules on the way in which governments should administer any import licensing requirements. Some import licensing procedures, indeed, are not intended to be quantitively restrictive at all; they may be intended only to facilitate the collection of statistical or other factual information. The objective of the rules was to try to ensure that the administration of import licensing did not in itself become a barrier to trade, or a means of discrimination over and above the effect avowedly intended by the restrictions themselves.

Agriculture

A second group of the package of agreements was concerned specifically with agriculture. Two of its three elements dealt with particular products—dairy products and meat. These were concerned principally with trying to improve procedures for exchange of information and for consultation, and not at all with buffer stocks or market organisation (though there were some protocols which aimed to establish minimum export prices for some dairy products). The third, which was the shortest in the whole package, purported to deal with the general question of negotiations on agriculture; but all that could be achieved was a recommendation to the Contracting Parties "to further develop active co-operation in the agricultural sector within an appropriate consultative framework," and that "the definition of this framework and its tasks be worked out as soon as possible." Given the weight that had been put on agriculture by the United States at the outset of the negotiations, and the interest of the agricultural countries like Australia and New Zealand, the agricultural content of the package can only be described as meagre.

Framework for the Conduct of International Trade

This title describes the focus of the third group in the package. Three separate topics were dealt with (though in one case without a conclusion) under this head. The first concerned the special position of the developing countries. The second was disputes procedure, and the third—the unfinished topic—was the use of safeguards.

On *Developing Countries*, the most important feature was the agreement to legitimise the grant of tariff preferences under the Generalised Schemes of Preference, differential non-tariff measures governed by codes negotiated under GATT auspices, and tariff preferences granted to one another by developing countries in regional or global trade arrangements, without the need for specific waivers case by case. This was provided for in an Enabling Clause, which in effect, even if not in form, was a substantive amendment of the GATT. The Clause also, inter alia, stated the "expectation" of developing countries that they "will be able to participate more fully in the framework of rights and obligations under the GATT with the progressive development of their economies and improvement in their trade situation". The "serious difficulties" of the "least developed countries" in this connection were recognised. This was the furthest the package went in the direction of what has come to be called "graduation"; in effect it continued the principle of self-election which was the basis of the Generalised Schemes of Preference, and the rather pious assumption that countries which chose to regard themselves as entitled to developing country status would similarly recognise the moment when they should renounce it.

The Understanding on *Notification, Consultation, Dispute Settlement and Surveillance* aimed to tighten up existing GATT procedures. Its principal advance was a requirement that governments should, in addition to their existing GATT obligations regarding publication and notification, "notify to the maximum extent possible the adoption of trade measures that affect the operation of the GATT". It also contained detailed provisions on the establishment and composition of panels to examine complaints, and rules covering the handling of panels' findings and follow up action on their recommendations. Attached to the Understanding was an "agreed description" of customary practice of the GATT in the dispute settlement field. The objective of the Understanding and this agreed description was to bring as much clarity and transparency as possible into the operation of the disputes settlement provisions, and to define more clearly the rights and obligations of individual countries.

On the use of *Safeguard Measures*, there were some limited agreements—on the one hand, to widen the grounds of justification of their use by developing countries for development purposes, and on the other to tighten procedures in relation to their use by developed countries for balance-of-payments purposes. One interesting feature of this "Declaration on Trade Measures taken for Balance of Payments Purposes" was the re-affirmation that such measures should not have the purpose of protecting a particular industry or sector, and the expression of "conviction that the stimulation of new investments that would not be economically viable in the absence of such measures should be avoided." However, the principal debate about safeguards was in relation to Article XIX of the GATT, which allows for emergency protective action to be taken when a product is being imported so as "to cause or threaten serious injury to domestic industry". On this issue, no agreement was reached; and it became the principal piece of unfinished business of the negotiations.

One of the main matters in this debate was the effort made by the European Community, with, in the end, the acquiescence, if not the support, of the United States and the other industrialised countries, to secure the right to use emergency safeguards "selectively"—ie against imports from particular countries—rather than, as in the generally accepted interpretation of Article XIX, non-discriminatorily. The developing countries saw in this the clear danger that, whatever limitations might be written into a safeguards code, the right to discriminate against particular sources of supply could easily mean that this became the normal and ready reaction of governments to pressure from sectoral interests facing competition from, especially, the newly industrialising countries.

Civil Aircraft

This Agreement was rather different in character from the rest of the non-tariff package. Somewhat surprisingly, it was a full blown Agreement for complete free trade in civil aircraft and components, to which all the major producing countries—the USA, the European Community, Japan, Sweden and Canada—were parties, to be effected by the elimination of all tariffs by 1st January 1980. The signatories also agreed that there should be "freedom for all purchasers to select supplies on the basis of commercial and technological factors", which implied that governments would not put pressure on their national airlines to buy from domestic producers.

Major Codes

Finally, there were "codes" on two subjects which go well beyond matters of procedure or technicalities, and are concerned with some of the central issues of the policies of governments towards industry and their implications for international trade. One dealt with government procurement, and the other with subsidies and counter-vailing duties.

The Agreement on *Government Procurement* went very much further than could have been expected in establishing the principles of non-discrimination and national treatment as between domestic products and suppliers and products and suppliers of other participating countries. It provides also a body of rules, in very considerable detail, for tendering procedures, to ensure their openness, transparency and equity. The key to this progress was secured by a formula of great ingenuity. The general principles laid down in the Agreement are potentially of universal application. But the actual coverage of the provisions is made a matter for negotiation. Each party specified a list of the entities whose purchases it was prepared to subject to the rules: there was thus a basis for negotiations on the respective offers, rather like the process of tariff bargaining. Moreover, the process is repeatable, without affecting the central features of the principles of the Agreement; and, indeed, there is provision for further negotiations to broaden the coverage and improve the Agreement, "especially by enlarging the lists of the entities subject to it," not later than the end of the third year of its life—ie before the end of 1983. These provisions certainly carried very much further forward the existing GATT provisions, which virtually allowed complete discrimination by governments in their own procurement activities.

The Agreement on *Subsidies and Countervailing Duties—*more formally the "Agreement on Interpretation and Application of Articles VI, XVI and XXIII of the GATT"—is a far more complex and difficult document; it could well have done with a dose of the "transparency" which has become a GATT catchword. The form in which the Code emerged was in very large measure shaped by the divergence of views between the United States and the European Community about the extent to which a code could go into detail in describing what sorts of subsidy should be prohibited, and what might be regarded as reasonable and acceptable.

One fundamental objective of the negotiations had been to secure a long sought change in United States legislation to modify the mandatory requirement, in US law, to impose countervailing duties against goods determined to have been subsidised, and to enable US practice to be brought into line with the GATT, and with the rest of the world, in determining whether there was injury to domestic industry before taking countervailing action. This was achieved. However, the text of the Agreement is in a number of ways ambivalent; and many observers have indeed considered that in some ways it may have weakened rather than strengthened the existing provisions of the GATT, by seeming to give explicit approval to the use of subsidies for a number of purposes of national policy. One of the purposes so approved is "the restructuring . . . of certain sectors, especially when this has become necessary by reason of changes in trade and economic policies, including international agreements resulting in lower barriers to trade." The implications of this seems to be that it might be acceptable for a signatory of the Code to seek to offset the effects of, say, a negotiated reduction in duties by direct subsidisation of domestic industry, so as to restore in that way the competitiveness which may have been lost. At the same time, the Code provided rather more substantial procedures for concilation, consultation and disputes adjudication. It was, therefore, a very open question, at the close of the Tokyo Round, in what direction the policies of governments would be affected by the Code, or whether it would make any difference at all.

III Trade Policy Developments, 1980-1982

The conclusion of the Tokyo Round engendered some guarded optimism for future international co-operation in the field of commercial policy. It would be difficult to say that events since then have done much to confirm that optimism. In considering these developments, we have to look at what has happened on at least three different levels. These are, first, *the declared intentions and avowals of governments;* secondly, *the nuts-and-bolts operations flowing directly from the agreements and understandings that made up the Tokyo package,* and taking place mainly inside the GATT machinery in Geneva; and thirdly, *the actions taken by Governments in the field of trade policy and the state of relations existing among the major trading countries, and generally in the world.*

GOVERNMENT DECLARATIONS

First, then, at the level of statements of high principle and intentions by Governments. The last five years or so have seen a greater institutionalisation of "summit meetings", and it is now taken for granted that there will be an annual meeting of the Heads of Government of the most powerful industrialised countries—the United States, Germany, France, Britain, Italy, Japan and Canada (and the President of the European Commission). Each of these meetings over recent years expressed itself powerfully in favour of liberal trade policy, and of the GATT and the open market system as the basis of the international commercial policy of all the countries participating, while also expressing concern and misgivings about the current dangers for the system of the continuing failure to achieve world economic recovery, and the protectionist pressures and measures that have occurred as a result. The summit meetings are supplemented by many regular meetings of Foreign Ministers, Ministers of Finance, and Ministers of Trade; perhaps the most important is the annual meeting of the Council of OECD at Ministerial level. The passage on trade in the Communiqué issued at the end of this meeting on 11th May 1982 can well stand for almost all these pronouncements, and its introductory paragraphs are worth quoting:

"19. The Ministers reiterated their full commitment, as expressed in the Declaration on trade policy of June 1980, to the open and multilateral trade system. They are fully aware of the contribution

13

that a further expansion of world trade can make to higher employment, improved productivity and rising income worldwide. They also noted that renewed non-inflationary growth would stimulate production and employment and thereby lessen protectionist pressures. The resumption of such growth could, however, be frustrated by a proliferation of trade restrictions and domestic policy measures having similar effects.

20. As a follow-up to the Declaration referred to above, Ministers reviewed developments in the trade policy field over the past year. Despite present economic difficulties, the international trading system has held up reasonably well. Ministers noted with concern, however, a further extension of protectionist pressures and trade measures, many of which are not governed by multilateral rules and disciplines, as well as the increase in bilateral tensions and disputes which affect the climate of trade relations. They recognised the dangers which these trends pose for the future of the system.

21. Ministers therefore agreed on the need for further joint efforts to resist protectionist pressures, and to resolve urgent short-term problems within the framework of the open and multilateral trading system. They are determined to maintain the credibility of this system at the present difficult juncture, and to work together with their trading partners on the longer-term issues which need to be tackled over the coming decade."

It is perhaps also worth noting that the matters which give concern—"trade measures . . . not governed by multilateral rules" and "bilateral tensions and disputes"—are referred to as though they were quite outside the responsibilities of the Ministers making the declaration.

DAY-TO-DAY WORK

At the other end of the scale is the work which goes on day-by-day in Geneva and elsewhere as, in effect, the continuing aftermath of the Tokyo Round negotiations—what I have called the nuts and bolts. The "package" was, for the most part, a blueprint which needed to be implemented partly by national legislation and national policy operation, partly by the establishment of mechanisms in Geneva, and work on them. The various topics can conveniently be looked at briefly in approximately the same order as they have been dealt with above; the discussion below sets out what has happened since 1979 on each of them.

Tariff Issues

The tariff reductions provided for in the negotiations have proceeded smoothly and without hitch. All the countries which made tariff undertakings have, so far as can be seen, gone ahead with them on time. Under pressure on other grounds, the Japanese have in fact accelerated their reduction programme by bringing forward to 1982 some cuts which they were not yet obliged to make. (But they are still being pressed to move further and faster on these lines).

However, some new tariff issues have emerged in the discussions that have gone on in Geneva. The first, concerning *Effective Tariff Levels*, arises from the fact that most countries, including all the industrial countries, organise their tariff levels so that higher rates are charged on manufactured goods than on intermediate products and semi-manufactures; and these in turn are higher rated than raw materials, which are very often admitted duty free. This structure—in the current jargon "tariff-escalation" or higher "effective tariffs"—means that the "effective" rate of protection given to the domestic manufacturing process itself is substantially higher than the "nominal" rate charged on the total value of imported competing products. In some cases—some Japanese tariff structures are quoted as outstanding examples—there is a sophisticated ascending scale of rates closely related to the degree of processing. The developing countries, who are for the most part raw materials producers and exporters, have represented strongly that this is a greater barrier to their ability to raise their level of industrialisation than has been accepted in previous rounds of negotiation; and that it should be re-examined.

The second issue is the consequence of the international work that has been done elsewhere—chiefly in the Customs Co-operation Council—on the *Harmonisation of Nomenclature* fo tariff purposes. The effect of implementing the results of this work will be to change the classification of a large number of items in the tariffs of a number of countries; and this will mean that tariff rates on many items will be changed, some upwards and some down. These changes will automatically involve a good deal of re-negotiation, especially where bound rates have to be increased. The Canadian tariff schedules may be particularly extensively affected, and this will raise questions between the United States and Canada.

Finally, there seems to be a certain amount of interest in some modest *Negotiation about Particular Items* in the tariffs of some countries. Taken altogether, it now seems possible that there may be more activity in tariff negotiation in the next two or three years than would have seemed likely at the time of the end of the Tokyo Round.

However, what has been happening, and what may happen, on tariffs is pretty well clear for all to see; indeed, the transparency and comparative certainty of the tariff system was one of the main reasons for its original acceptance in the GATT as the only legitimate method of protecting domestic industries. What has been happening in relation to the Tokyo Round codes is less easily ascertainable.

The Non-Tariff Agreements

The first question here is the *Meaning of Accession to the Codes,* given the fact that many countries which are contracting parties to the GATT—especially those other than the major industrialised ones—have signed only a few of the ten codes, or quite often none of them. Table A (pages 18-19) illustrates this disparity as of mid-1982.

The result, on the face of it, is a somewhat patchy network of obligations in a two-tier system. On the one hand, there is the GATT itself, in which, in principle, all the Contracting Parties carry the same set of rights and obligations each towards each, though with some special provisions for the developing countries, a term so far undefined. On the other hand, there are the Codes, each with its own group of signatories, where, broadly speaking, the OECD countries, with a few others in relation to some of the Codes, have subscribed to some additional rules, principles, and procedures, vis-a-vis one another, but not for non-signatories. This is, of course, an untidy situation. It is made all the more so, in theory at all events, because countries which are members of the GATT but do not choose to become signatories of a Code, may still be able to rest on their right, under Article 1 of the GATT, to most-favoured-nation treatment over much (though not quite all) of the matters covered by the Codes. So far, however, this untidiness does not seem to have created difficulty in practice; but some aspects of it could become troublesome.

For example, the United States denies the benefits of its adherence to "injury test" to non-signatories of the Agreement on subsidies and countervailing.

For each of the Codes, the first task was to satisfy the initial procedural requirements—to set up the Committee of Signatories (a separate one for each), put in place the rules of procedure (mostly following a common form) and establish the machinery of operation. In most cases, there has also already been some initial review of the extent to which signatory countries have completed implementing legislation, where necessary, or other implementation procedures. This has been done largely by question and answer, in which the United States and the Scandinavians seem to have been the most active operators. There have been some laggards in the process of bringing domestic legislation into line: the French and Italian legislation has only recently been completed, and the Europeans seem to believe that there are still some deficiencies in US implementation.

The *Customs Valuation Code* came into force on 1st January 1981, a year later than most of the others, because of the time needed to make appropriate arrangements. There seems to be general consent that it is working well, and it is estimated that probably more than 90% of all valuations for tariff purposes, in signatory countries, have been made at transaction (ie invoice) values. We have no basis for comparing this with what may have happened previously; but there has not been much, if any, complaint from traders, who would be adversely affected if it were not working well.

The *Standards Code* also seems to have started reasonably well. Some 500 international standards have been notified. However, the procedures are very complex, and no doubt could be improved. It also remains true that substantial complaints are still made about the way in which some countries operate local standards requirements so as to give them the effect of a non-tariff barrier. If there is substance in these complaints, the Standards Code has not yet been at all effective in mitigating them.

Much the same can be said about *Import Licencing Procedures*. In both cases, there are vociferous complaints, especially from Europe, about the Japanese. But it is by no means clear whether the failure to make a specific case under the codes is because the Codes' provisions need to be strengthened, or because the complaints do not have sufficient substance.

TABLE A

THE ACCESSION OF GATT MEMBER COUNTRIES TO PRINCIPAL TOKYO ROUND AGREEMENTS
as of July 1, 1982

A = Accepted.
The country has formally agreed to be bound by the agreement.

AR = Accepted with Reservations.
The country has agreed to be bound by the agreement except with respect to certain obligations of it.

SSR = Signed Subject to Ratification.
The country has accepted the agreement but domestic ratification procedures have not been completed and an instrument of ratification has not been deposited with the GATT Secretariat.

GATT MEMBER COUNTRY / AGREEMENT	Tariff	Standards	Procurement	Subsidies	Meat	Dairy	Customs Valuation	Import Licensing	Aircraft	Anti-Dumping
DEVELOPED COUNTRIES										
European Community	A	A	A*	A*	A*	A*	A*	A*	A	A*
BELGIUM	A	A	A*	A*	A*	A*	A*	A*	A	A*
DENMARK	A	A	A*	A*	A*	A*	A*	A*	A	A*
FRANCE	A	A	A*	A*	A*	A*	A*	A*	A	A*
WEST GERMANY	A	A	A*	A*	A*	A*	A*	A*	A	A*
GREECE	A	SSR	A*	A*	A*	A*	A*	A*	SSR	A*
IRELAND	A	A	A*	A*	A*	A*	A*	A*	A	A*
ITALY	A	A	A*	A*	A*	A*	A*	A*	SSR	A*
LUXEMBOURG	A	A	A*	A*	A*	A*	A*	A*	A	A*
NETHERLANDS	A	A	A*	A*	A*	A*	A*	A*	A	A*
UNITED KINGDOM	A	A	A*	A*	A*	A*	A*	A*	A	A*
Other OECD										
AUSTRALIA	A	A		A	A	A		A		
AUSTRIA	A	A	A	A	A	A	A	A	A	A
CANADA	A	A	A	A	A		AR	A	A	A
FINLAND	A	A	A	A	A	A	A	A		A
ICELAND	A									
JAPAN	A	A	A	A	A	A	A	A	A	A
NEW ZEALAND	A	A		A	A	A	A	A		
NORWAY	A	A	A	A	A	A	A	A	A	A
SPAIN	A	A		A			A			A
SWEDEN	A	A		A	A	A	A	A	A	A
SWITZERLAND	A	A	A	A	A	A	A	A	A	A
UNITED STATES	A	A	A	A	A	A	A	A	A	A
YUGOSLAVIA	A	SSR		SSR	A		SSR	A		A

*Accepted on behalf of all countries of the European Community.

AGREEMENT / GATT MEMBER COUNTRY	Tariff	Standards	Procurement	Subsidies	Meat	Dairy	Customs Valuation	Import Licensing	Aircraft	Anti Dumping
DEVELOPED COUNTRIES *cont*										
Other developed countries										
CZECHOSLOVAKIA	A							A		A
HUNGARY	A	A			A	A	A	A		A
ISRAEL	SSR									
POLAND	A									
RUMANIA	A	A			A	A	A	A	A	A
SOUTH AFRICA	A				A	A	A			
DEVELOPING COUNTRIES										
Newly industrialising countries										
ARGENTINA	A	SSR			A	SSR	SSR	SSR		
BRAZIL	A	A		A	A		AR			A
HONG KONG		A	A	A			A	A	A	A
INDIA	A			A			A	A		A
KOREA	A	A		A			A			
SINGAPORE	A	A	A							
Other developing countries										
CHILE	A	A		A			A			
DOMINICAN REPUBLIC	A									
EGYPT	A	SSR		SSR	SSR	SSR		SSR	SSR	SSR
INDONESIA	A									
IVORY COAST	A									
JAMAICA	A									
MALAYSIA	A									
PAKISTAN	A	A		A				A		A
PERU	A									
PHILIPPINES		A						A		
RWANDA		A								
URUGUAY	A			A	A	A				
ZAIRE	A									

Source: GATT Document L/4914/Rev.5/Add. 9. as compiled by the US Trade Representative.

The *Agricultural Arrangements* on exchange and evaluation of information have fulfilled their functions without causing any great stir. There does not seem to have been any significant activity on the agricultural "framework". There has however, been the innovation of holding an "agricultural day" of discussions each time the Group of 18 meets.

The free trade arrangements for *Civil Aircraft* have been brought into force as envisaged. It has been agreed that the provisions of the Codes on Standards and on Subsidies should also be applied to work in Civil Aircraft, and there have been discussions in the Committee of Signatories on a number of issues of interpretation, such as product coverage and tariff nomenclature. There is a continuing area of potential difficulty in relation to the extent of governments' influence over national airlines, but no cases on this have come to a head yet.

It is too early to say whether the *Code on Government Procurement* has led to a significant change in trade patterns or buying habits. But there seems to be agreement that there have at least been some broadening and greater transparency in procedures, and that progress, if slow, is being made. The Committee of Signatories has begun to discuss the possible extension of entities to be brought within the provisions, as part of the review to be concluded by the end of 1983.

The outcome of the continuing debate about the problems of *developing countries* will best be dealt with in the general discussion about the future, and the same applies to *safeguards*.

This leaves to be described what has happened on the *Subsidies Code* and in general on subsidies and countervailing. As might have been expected, this has proved to be the most difficult area of operation in the whole field. There has, of course, been fairly calm continuing work in the Code's Committee ·of Signatories, dealing with countries' legislation and implementing regulations; according to the GATT's report, "attention has been drawn to some shortcomings" in some cases. It would be very difficult to suppose, however, that the Code has made any difference at all, so far, at any rate, to governments' policies on the use of subsidies. The United States has made something of a drive to try to get judgements on the subsidy practices of a number of countries, especially on the European Community's Common Agricultural Policy. Some of the cases put forward—wheat flour, sugar, poultry, pasta, canned fruit, and others—have been taken under the procedures of the Code, some under the rules of the GATT. The outcome has yet to be seen, as the cases are still embedded in the GATT process, but there is no indication that the Community is in the least ready to accept that its practice is at fault. The difference in philosophy which underlay the US and European positions during the Tokyo Round negotiations (see page 11) still persists; and this issue seems set to become an embittering influence in commercial policy relations. The Committee has also conducted, on the basis of notifications from countries, a semi-annual review of the use of countervailing duties, from which it emerges that this is virtually entirely a North American practice. The wider significance of this divide between the US and the Community on subsidies, and in some similar respects in relation to anti-dumping activity under United States legislation, will be discussed below.

This account suggests that the activity resulting directly from the Tokyo Round is mixed. It is fair to say that in some areas the direction of policy has been moved towards greater openness; but that in some others—and especially agriculture and subsidies—the results have so far been at best neutral.

GOVERNMENT ACTIONS AND INTERNATIONAL RELATIONS

We can turn now to the broad third level of trade policy developments during 1980-1982—the actions of governments, the state of relations among the major trading countries, and some other aspects of international trade policy development.

Commentators on the international trade scene agree almost completely that, in spite of the clear statements of Heads of Government at the summits and of other high level meetings, which pledge allegiance to the liberal trade system—(along the lines quoted in Chapter II)—there has in fact been a considerable re-emphasis on bilateral balancing of trade, and the pursuit of policies of various kinds which, in one way or another, signify a revival of economic nationalism. Taken together, these tendencies must, directly or indirectly, have damaging effects on the free movement of international trade.

Although there have been a few manifestations of bilateralism as a general phenomenon—which have found their most obvious expression in a number of Bills about "reciprocity" put forward in the US Congress—its chief importance is in relation to trade with Japan, and it should be considered in that context. The other forms of trade distorting actions are, on the whole, not protectionist measures of the traditional kind. They have included:

(i) outside the purely commercial field—direct or indirect financial assistance or subsidies (advances, low interest loans, tax concessions, and excessively generous terms of export credit insurances) including measures intended to safeguard jobs in ailing firms;

(ii) manipulation of exchange rate policy as an inducement to influence trade flows;

(iii) a variety of trade measures, including import surveillance, and more widespread use of technical and administrative require-ments—visas, marks of origin, and frontier and customs clearance procedures;

(iv) a greater readiness to respond to complaints about competition regarded by domestic industry as "unfair"—eg. simplification of procedures and speedier action on anti-dumping applications;

(v) —far and away the most important—broad scale arrangements which affect very important industrial sectors and cover a large part of the trade in those sectors. The approach is different from the conventional use of emergency safeguards measures. It is tailored to the particular sector concerned, and may sometimes directly involve interference with cross border transactions—through "orderly market arrangements", or voluntary export restraints. In this form, it will often result from operations which do not overtly involve governments, but appear to be arrangements arrived at between the private interests concerned. But very frequently, the actions taken involve some kind of domestic policy which avoids direct intervention in international trade process, although its effects will be felt there.

It is this kind of activity which the Director General of the GATT had particularly in mind when he discussed the tendency towards "sectoralism" in trade policy in a speech at Hamburg on 5th March 1982[3]. Similarly, much of the discussion which has gone on in the OECD over the past three years about how to deal with the problems

---

3 This speech is reproduced in Appendix I.

of "structural adjustment" has been concerned to direct the minds of governments to the dangers involved in short term, *ad hoc*, intervention by governments.

Perhaps the most important new dimension in thinking about international commercial policy for many years is this growing recognition of the relationship between two areas of government activity traditionally regarded as separate. One is the international trade system. The other is government interventions in the day-to-day conduct of business by means of either "industrial policy" (meaning the attempt by government to influence the whole general pattern and direction of the industrial activity and development in its country) or, more narrowly, "structural adjustment policy" (meaning the effort to influence the way in which the industrial pattern meets particular pressures for change). Until recently indeed, there was an inclination to see such industrial policy, especially under the heading of structural adjustment, as a respectable, even perhaps desirable, *alternative to protection*. The proliferation of activity of this kind in recent years, however, has demonstrated how near it comes to being a clearly alternative *method of protection*, especially when it is used as a means of preserving existing structures which would otherwise succumb to competition from either changed technology or more efficient competitors, either at home or from other countries. It is, no doubt, also the case that the use of such policies has been much enhanced precisely because the degree of protection offered by tariffs has been worn down by successive reductions in the course of the negotiations of the last thirty years. To that extent, policies which aim to offset the effect of tariff reductions might be seen as mistaken on two counts. First, they would, in effect, be trying to nullify the reciprocity of the negotiation which has included a particular tariff cut (and thus cheating on the bargain that had been struck). Secondly, they would implicitly be denying the principle on which the whole liberal trade system rests—that the maximisation of international trade, by increasing the area of competition and of freedom of choice, contributes to a more efficient use of resources world-wide.

This line of thought has become influential, especially in the OECD. However, Governments have been put under great pressures by the long persistence of economic depression in the world; and they have committed themselves deeply to their electorates to accept direct responsibility for the general level of employment (and often for the survival of particular lines of production and even of particular firms). All this has imposed increasing interventions in more and more sectors of their economies. These pressures, which may push governments to act in ways which may be inconsistent with the open trade system, and sometimes in overt or covert contravention of the rules of the GATT, arise out of the very real, and potent, forces and changes in the world. We have already noted that the changes that took place in the relative economic positions of the United States and its major trading partners, over the first two decades after the establishment of the post war international monetary and trade system, were followed by disturbed international relations at the beginning of the 1970s. This might have been weathered without undue strain had other conditions in the world been calm. But this was far from being so. The oil crises and the persistent and apparently unrelenting world economic recession have imposed great strains on all countries, event the strongest. These strains have been all the more difficult for the older industrialised countries to bear in face of the emergence of new and powerful competitors in world trade— first from the apparently uncontrollable surge of Japanese exports in a few sectors, then from a number of what have come to be called the "newly industrialising countries", again in a few sectors, and finally from the full scale development of highly advanced and innovative technology from Japan. Even within the older countries themselves, the advance of technology—which once would have been welcomed as unreservedly implying a general increase in living standards—is now often feared as likely to reduce the prospects for employment.

All these forces would have been absorbed with much less difficulty and disturbance in an atmosphere of expanding activity and increasing productivity; and in such an atmosphere the open market trade system would itself have made its own additional contribution to the potential increase in world prosperity by promoting the optimal utilisation of world resources. In a period of slow-growth and faltering progress, however, the changes that need to be made to accommodate both new technology and new competitors are very painful, and certainly entail substantial social costs; and they are made all the more difficult if the pace at which these forces grow is much more rapid than has been the historic pattern. It is not difficult to understand the strength of the pressures for resistance to change, or to see why this leads to pressures on government to take actions which, it is believed—rightly or wrongly—will stave off the need for change, or at any rate moderate its pace.

So long as governments, whether individually or collectively—and the major responsibility for this must rest with the major industrial countries—fail to find constructive answers to the problems involved in restoring world economic expansion, the pressures for detailed intervention, including measures which may restrict trade, are bound to remain strong. The agreements of the Tokyo Round have not, in the event, slowed down these tendencies; if anything, as the Director General of the GATT observed, they have quickened in the last two years. This was the principal factor in the discussions which led to the decision for the November 1982 Ministerial Meeting of the GATT, with the recommendation of the Group of Eighteen emphasising the need for a "strong *political* commitment" to the multilateral trading system. Meanwhile, however, relations between major trading countries have become increasingly acrimonious, to the point of real danger of serious trade conflict, especially between the European Community and the United States. We shall look at this in the next chapter.

IV National Stances and International Conflicts, 1982

Both the earlier Reports in this series made it clear that the world pattern of international commercial policy was very heavily, indeed decisively, affected by the actions of the United States and the European Community. They cannot, of course, dictate to other countries. But their actions and reactions must set the tone for the general conduct of world trade and trade relations; and in any negotiations or international debate, no general agreement will be possible unless agreement can be reached between them. It is inevitable, therefore, that an account of national stances should concentrate on what is known of the policies, attitudes and intentions of the two major commercial powers, and on their relations with each other and with the rest of the world.

Given this fact, it is not surprising that the characteristic condition of current international trade and economic relations is of continuing, and in some respects rising, tension. Certainly there are very substantial, and, unfortunately, increasing frictions in relations between the United States and the Community, as well as significant tensions elsewhere in the world picture—US/Japan; Europe/Japan; US/Canada; Europe/the major agricultural producers; and between the industrialised countries and the developing countries, especially those that qualify as newly industrialising countries[4]. In large measure, these North-South tensions centre on a number of specific industries—textiles, other traditional consumer goods (footwear, cutlery, etc.), consumer electronics, steel, shipbuilding. In many cases, these difficulties stem from the strains resulting from domestic economic depression and its transmission to world trade. But they reflect also the facts that many industries in the older industrial countries have not yet sufficiently adapted themselves to competition from new sources, and that structural adjustment is impeded by the continuing effects of cyclical depression.

In this climate, the spectacle of the two dominating economic powers at serious odds with each other over many aspects of both economic and commercial policy, and embroiled in disputes over the alleged damage to each other's trade through their respective actions, can hardly induce a strong measure of respect for the international trade system in the minds of the rest of the world.

---

4 These are discussed more fully in Neil McMullen: *The Newly Industrializing Countries: Adjusting to Success*, British-North American Committee, October 1982.

THE UNITED STATES AND THE EUROPEAN COMMUNITY

The US Administration, and even more its politicians and public opinion, see the United States as the original inspirer and long time defender of the liberal trade system and its embodiment in the GATT. Surveying the world scene in the early 1980's, they also see the United States as now the only staunch and sincere adherent of the system, and as the standard bearer in a battle to restore and reinvigorate the international rule of law.

The US political system, with the shared responsibility of the Administration and Congress, makes it much easier to observe what is in the minds of American policy makers than is the case in most other countries; much of the process goes on in public, and particularly in statements by spokesmen to committees of Congress. A synthesis of some of these statements, and other public pronouncements, suggests that the American presentation of their position would be along the following lines.

The US View

The firm commitment of the United States to the principles of the GATT means that it must continue to fight for those principles; in the course of doing so, it must also insist that its trading partners, and especially its major partners, do likewise. The United States must, therefore, take an aggressive stand wherever and whenever it sees other countries failing to observe their obligations. As far as Europe is concerned, the Community has always co-operated closely with the United States. Indeed, this was successful in holding protectionism in check through the 1970's, and especially through the disturbed conditions created by the oil shock, and in bringing the Tokyo Round to a successful conclusion.

But the fruitful continuance of this co-operation requires that both sides live up to their obligations. It will fail if either tries to escape its problems by shifting the burden to the other. The continuing pressures of industrial depression seem to be pushing the Community, or individual members, into attempts to insulate some elements of their economy from foreign competition—especially from Japan and the developing countries—and to increasing subsidies to exporters. Moreover, as successive negotiations have peeled away traditional trade barriers, they have revealed deeper-seated obstacles. In the world as a whole—and by implication in Europe at least to some extent—tariff reductions have simply served to raise more subtle barriers to protect particular sectors; and many devices have emerged which still prevent the functioning of free markets.

The European reaction to these pressures and tendencies produces some specific areas of conflict between the Community and the United States.

The first of these is in relation to *Agriculture*, where the respective policies, as the Americans view them, are inspired by quite different philosophies. The United States sees itself as interfering as little as possible in international markets; it takes surplus US production off the domestic market but does not dampen world prices by subsidising exports. It thus contributes to world food stability and international price stability. The Community's policy, by contrast, in the US view, is based on high price supports, which almost inevitably produce surpluses; and these prices are bolstered by variable levies at the border. The surpluses then enter the world market at subsidised prices, causing artificially stimulated large-scale community exports of wheat, sugar and meat. This in its turn limits market opportunities for countries like the United States, whose exports get no subsidy.

The United States recognises the social and political importance of the Community's Common Agricultural Policy, but sees these aspects of it as converting it into a policy which leads to exports based on extensive subsidies. It is disturbed also because from time to time the Community considers curbing agricultural imports from others into its own market—for example soya beans and feed grain substitutes. The United States must therefore, it contends, defend its own interests and rights. For this reason, and also because it wants to defend the principles on which the international system is based, the United States has embarked on an intensive series of complaints—wheat, flour, sugar, poultry, pasta, canned foods—in the GATT against the Community.

This formulation of the US view of the Common Agricultural Policy, it must be remembered, is by no means new. Indeed, most of the elements in it go back a very long time indeed; as long ago as 1971, I wrote that the US charges against the CAP were that "It contravenes the GATT; it is highly protectionist—more so than even a quota system; it blunts and distorts the US natural competitive advantage in important agriculture commodities, and it damages the interest and earning power of many developing countries; it is aggressive, predatory and subsidised in exports to third markets[5]."

The second specific area of US/European Community conflict is in relation to the *Steel* industry. Here also, there is a long history of friction, which recent US action, in imposing countervailing duties, has now brought to a head. The US view stresses that while both the European and US steel industries are in the process of substantial restructuring, the latter does this with its own resources, but the European steel industry benefits from central planning and large and continuing infusions of public funds. This difference has caused dispute over "subsidised" steel exports from the Community countries to the United States. Under US law, any domestic industry can initiate the process which may lead to countervailing duty suits in the courts. The US government wants to see a modernised, healthy steel industry on both sides of the Atlantic; but it cannot ask domestic industry to wait while subsidised imports harm its own efforts to rationalise. Washington maintains that it will certainly ensure that US procedures, on any suits, are scrupulously fair, but it is obliged to act in accordance with US law.

Of course, the United States does not want to see any of these conflicts embitter overall relations with Europe. On the contrary it wants to restore transatlantic co-operation, so as to make possible the vigorous functioning of the international system. It will not, the Administration says, allow frustration with GATT's seeming inability to deal with new forms of trade barriers and distortions to justify US abandonment of the commitment to open trade. But it must secure adequate "reciprocal" advantage from the system.

The Community View

It is usually less easy to get as authoritative a view of the European Community position on any topic as the American. It is particularly difficult to get a Community view on general issues, because this has to emerge from negotiation among the member states. However, it is possible to construct a fairly full picture of the current Community position on particular issues, especially on agriculture and steel, from recent statements from the Director General of the European Commission concerned with trade policy[6]. On trade issues, the Commission is the negotiating arm of the Community.

---

5 Sidney Golt: *Is World Trade Threatened?* The Banker, London, September 1971.

6 See especially Sir Roy Denman's speech at Houston, May 1982. *European Community News* No. 11, 1982, May 18th 1982.

As might be expected, the Community does not see the situation in at all the same way as the United States does. Its approach to the international trade system, it would say, is more pragmatic and less based on doctrinal considerations; its style is less missionary and evangelistic. But in practice, it contends, the United States is itself quite as cavalier about the rules when its own interests are involved.

As regards *Agriculture* in particular, the United States itself secured, as long ago as 1955, the ability to disregard the rules of the GATT, so that it can impose what controls it likes on imports of cotton, sugar, dairy products, etc. And several US practices—the DISC system, in force since 1972, which the Community regards as an export subsidy, and on which the United States has not been willing to accept GATT jurisdiction; government to government agreements on milk products; drawback arrangements on sugar—are, in the Community view, incompatible with the GATT. As for agricultural subsidies there is clearly a basic difference of perception. But it is not the case, as the US seems to be implying, that the international rules condemn agricultural subsidies and require their removal. In fact, the Tokyo Round confirmed and elaborated the long standing rule that agricultural subsidies are permitted providing that these do not lead to any member of the GATT obtaining more than an equitable share of world trade.

Nor is the Community alone in giving aid to farmers. US suggestions that the cost of farm support in the Community is 40% higher than that in the US are misleading. A true comparison has to look beyond direct central budget support to other policies also—policies affecting land, production costs, direct and indirect taxation, transport costs—and, in the United States to State budgets as well as Federal. If like is compared with like, farm support in the United States and in the Community is of much the same order of magnitude. When all this is translated into what is happening in world trade, the Community sees the United States as a more aggressive trader (and quotes the Secretary of Agriculture as saying that his Department is working aggressively to stimulate long-term growth of exports of US farm products). Certainly Community exports of wheat doubled between 1969-1970 and 1980-1981; but its share of world trade fell from 16.6% to 14.9%. Over the same period US exports increased 2½ times, and their share of world trade rose from 38.4% to 44.8%. So the Community rejects the US view that its Common Agricultural Policy produces "harmful" export subsidies, which justify the US in seeking a "plan and timetable for their elimination". That goes far beyond the Tokyo Round agreement on the "equitable share of the world market" as the relevant criterion.

On *Steel*, the Community feels that what is happening is a campaign of harassment against European exporters. Insofar as there are allegations of dumping, nothing in the GATT states that dumping is illegal. What the GATT does provide is the possibility to impose anti-dumping duties if dumping exists to a sufficient extent to cause material injury. As regards countervailing, the Department of Commerce's findings are rejected as strong on allegations but weak on evidence, and as indicating that the American legislation opens the door to harassment on a scale which amounts to a non-tariff barrier.

In these circumstances, the Community sees the *US Recourse to the GATT* for its complaints in so many cases—the list quoted on page 27—as excessive and risking overloading the dispute settlement process in the GATT to the point of destruction, and its action on steel as intemperate and unjustified. By contrast, the Community points to its own resistance to pressure for import restrictions on US exports of petrochemicals, which European producers regarded as made possible by the way in which US government action has depressed—artificially, as the Europeans see it—the price of US natural gas; the European industry had been firmly told that unless material injury could be demonstrated, there was no action to be taken under the GATT. However, in the face of these US actions the Community has felt obliged to re-open its complaint in the GATT against the US DISC scheme, and to claim compensation for its effects.

It must be clear from this account that the conflicts between the United States and the Community on trade policy are now escalating dangerously, and that only a substantial political effort, and a strong economic up-turn on both sides, can improve the situation.

THE US/EUROPEAN COMMUNITY AND JAPAN

If the United States and Europe are seriously at odds with each other on some issues, they are much closer together, in substance if not in action, in their attitudes to Japan.

The Community View

On this front, it is the European Community's position which is better documented, since in 1982 it carried its differences with Japan to the point of a formal complaint under Article XXIII of the GATT. Under this Article, one Contracting Party can complain against another on the grounds that the benefits it is entitled to expect under the Agreement are being "nullified or impaired" as a result of the other's failure to carry out its obligations, or as the result of the application by the other of any measure, whether or not it conflicts with the provisions of the Agreement, or as the result of any other situation. The Article provides for consultation between the parties with a view to resolving the complaint, followed if necessary by collective adjudication which may authorise counteraction by the complainant, if the complaint is justified. There is no precedent for the sort of general action against the whole Japanese trading system which the Community has made, and, depending on the outcome, the case which is still at an early stage of consideration, could be of very great importance indeed[7].

The background to the present state of relations between both the European Community and the United States (and for that matter Japan's other industrialised country trading partners) on the one hand, and Japan on the other, has in fact barely altered since the following description of it which appeared in the first Report[8] in this series:

"A special position in the negotiations for Japan . . . derives not solely from the volume of Japanese trade as a proportion of world trade, impressive and important as that is, but from the speed of its growth and the seemingly (during a crucial period) uncontainable character of its competitive power, and the implications this appeared to have for a philosophy of international commercial policy based on the freedom of the market.

The scale and surge of Japanese penetration were all the more significant by contrast with the difficulty of exporting to

---

7 Appendix III contains an extract from the European Communities representations to the Japanese Government on this subject.

8 Sidney Golt: *The GATT Negotiations, 1973-1975;* BNAC London, Washington and Montreal, 1974.

Japan, only partly to be explained by tariff and other barriers . . .
Japan will need to convince the other participants—and on this
the United States and the Community will be aligned, not
opposed—*first,* that her own acceptance of, and adherence to,
GATT obligations is absolute and that she will abandon
whatever vestiges of protective quota restrictions remain;
secondly, that the contribution to the pool of tariff reduction
and other measures of liberalisation which Japan will make
or has already made provide a very full measure of reciprocity
against the concessions of the other participants; and *thirdly—*
and most difficult—that the Japanese system is not so naturally
impenetrable, even without formal barriers, that genuine
reciprocity of treatment is in fact incapable of achievement."

The Japanese have clearly failed to convince their trading
partners on the third of these points; and the position on this aspect
is exactly the same in the United States as in Europe. In both places
a quite significant school of thought holds that the Japanese system,
and indeed the whole Japanese way of life, habit of thought, and
economic and commercial structure, are so naturally and unshakeably
inward-looking, that the GATT principles, based on the assumption
that commercial decisions, and consumer's choice, will be decided
by market considerations, cannot apply to trading with Japan. The
US and Community governments would not go quite so far as
this; but there has no doubt been some element of reluctance, perhaps
more marked in Europe than in the United States, to feel as full a
sense of common participation in a mutually advantageous trade
partnership with Japan as with other industrialised countries.
This may have derived in part from the pervasiveness of the
concept of "Japan Inc" which has been presented over the last 10
years or so—the idea that there was a highly concentrated and
irresistible partnership of Japanese industry and government, with
carefully planned and centrally directed strategies of production
and, especially, export marketing.

Whatever the reasons, it is in relation to trade with Japan
that the revived emphasis on bilateral trade balancing has been most
potent, and where bilateral arrangements for restriction of trade—in
particular voluntary export restraints and "orderly marketing arrangements"—have been pursued most vigorously. In the Community,
most, if not all, member countries have either imposed, openly or

covertly, restrictions on a number of items imported from Japan—most notably automobiles and television sets—or have supported negotiations between the industries concerned to produce the same result. Meanwhile, the United States had used similar measures, but on a smaller scale. At the same time, Europeans and Americans have complained that Japan still maintains non-tariff barriers—exercised in concealed ways and by not easily recognised administrative methods—which seriously impede their exports. The Japanese Government has tried, in recent months, to find ways to satisfy the pressures to get rid of surviving instruments of protection; but it has still failed to persuade the rest of the world of the openness of the Japanese market. However the Community has set itself to go beyond this objective. It seeks to persuade Japan to modify its trading and economic policies and to achieve a more balanced integration of the Japanese economy with that of its main industrialised partners. What has to be redressed, the Community says, is the root cause, ie Japanese low import propensity. Removal of border barriers is welcome; but, the Community insists, the Japanese government should actively promote imports. She should also pursue a policy of effective moderation in exports in sectors where an increase would cause significant problems, such as automobiles, colour television sets and tubes, and some machine tools. And the policy areas covered should also go beyond trade to macro-economic policies and the development of the yen as an international trading currency. Japan's policies must take account of her international responsibilities. It was on the basis of these considerations that the Community launched its invocation of Article XXIII of the GATT.

The US View

The United States has not made so far-reaching a *demarche* as Europe, but in both the Administration and Congress the general trend of thought would certainly concur substantially with the Community analysis. Much of the discussion about "reciprocity" is clearly based on what is seen as the problem of Japan. The argument is that the President's present authority on trade relations does not provide him with sufficient power to cope with Japanese administrative practices and policies, and that some extension of the law is needed, under which special measures could be taken against countries which were designated as not offering "substantially equivalent commercial opportunities" to American trade. The US Administration has now moved towards defusing the "reciprocity" issue: but Congressional support for action against Japan might well press for the United States to go even further than the European Community has done so far.

The Japanese reaction to all this has been fairly calm. The government has tried to demonstrate its readiness to do much to open up the market so far as this is within its power. It has, *inter alia*, accelerated its Tokyo Round tariff reductions, and set up machinery to look into complaints about unfair administrative treatment of imports. Japanese industry itself, through its representative organisation, the Keidanren, has made recommendations to the government for additional measures of liberalisation. But the basic Japanese answer to the Europeans and Americans remains that if Japanese consumers prefer to buy Japanese goods, they do so for the same reason as do many Americans and Europeans—that they are better and cheaper; and that this is simply consistent with the principles on which the GATT is founded.

In taking this line, the Japanese can claim to have at least some measure of support from the Director General of the GATT. In the speech already quoted[9], he also said the following:

> "Every government has a need to find scapegoats when the effects of its policies turn out not to be the ones it has expected and announced. Thus, the problem of competition with Japan has begun to assume the proportions of a crisis, though in reality it is only a symptom of the more general problem—and Japan is only the forerunner of a series of highly efficient newcomers on the world markets for manufacture. The West appears mesmerised by the spectacular productivity of Japanese industry—but the farsighted Japanese are already worrying about Korea, India and, in 10 years perhaps, China.
>
> I know that exporting to Japan poses special problems. The Japanese Government itself has recognised that there are things it should do to facilitate the entry of foreign goods, and has begun to implement them. This is to be welcomed, but is not a panacea: we must not forget the important truth which Ludwig Erhard preached in the 1950s, that an economy

9. See appendix I

becomes more, not less, efficient as it opens itself up to imports. A better functioning of the international monetary system, which would enable Japanese society, through a higher exchange rate, to reap the benefits of its efficiency in the form of cheaper imports, would greatly reduce these tensions. But in my view the only permanent solution to the so-called "Japanese problem" is for the Western economies to raise their productivity to Japanese levels, to accept the challenge. It is possible to exclude more efficient producers from one's domestic market, at great political and economic cost; but the corollary is acceptance of defeat in third markets."

These are certainly brave words from an international civil servant. But they are not likely to quench the Brussels/Washington/Tokyo debate. A series of quadrilateral meetings were launched in 1981 to discuss trade policy problems in which the United States, the Commission and the Japanese have been joined by the Canadians, and these are likely to continue as a periodic forum of discussion. These meetings have served, so far as can be seen, to offer another occasion for all the participants to say the same things in each other's presence as they have previously said separately.

THE UNITED STATES AND CANADA

There must always be a very large measure of special relationship in economic matters between the United States and Canada. The bilateral trading and investment relationship is the largest and most extensive linking any two countries in the world. In 1981 two-way trade between them approached $87 billion, accounting for more than 70% of Canada's and almost 20% of US total international trade.

Far and away the bulk of this trade, and of the enormous network of other economic transactions between the two countries, continues to flow without difficulty. Indeed, as much as 76% of Canadian exports to the United States, and 70% of US exports to Canada, were passed duty-free. However, there have recently emerged several areas of quite sharp friction between the two governments, arising chiefly from what the United States sees as unfair and discriminatory treatment. The chief cause of this ill feeling arises from Canadian efforts to impose conditions of various kinds on foreign investment in Canada, as part of its general policy aimed partly at ensuring a high degree of Canadian control, or at least participation, in development (especially in the energy field), and partly at securing what it sees as tangible benefits for the Canadian economy in the way of employment, use of Canadian components or materials, and exports.

The second of these aims is pursued through the Foreign Investment Review Agency (FIRA), which requires those seeking to enlarge existing investments or to make new ones to enter into discussion about their plans and prospects before permission to do so is given. The Agency, as the United States sees it, frequently requires investors to sign legally enforceable agreements which specify when they must buy Canadian goods. This the US regards as violating the provisions of the GATT—Article III—requiring equal treatment in the application of governmental regulations between imported and domestic products. FIRA may also require undertakings from foreign firms about targets for exports out of their Canadian production, which the Americans (and European investors also) see as distorting trade flows. FIRA may also impose limitations or prohibitions on distribution in Canada.

For their part, the Canadians regard these complaints as exaggerated and basically unreasonable. They point to the enormous weight of US investment in Canada, much of which is entirely controlled by the US interests concerned. They feel that they are thoroughly justified in trying to ensure that the national interests of Canada are taken into account in that expansion of foreign investment. But, they say, for the most part FIRA operates by seeking to get promises from investors to use their best endeavours to look to Canadian sources where possible, and that the more or less standard undertaking which foreign firms commonly offer contains the proviso that Canadian sources must be competitive in terms of price, quality and availability. The principal factors in the disallowance of about 15% of foreign investment proposals have, in fact, been based on quite different considerations than these—most often the incompatibility of proposals with the government's general policies on the orderly restructuring of some sectors of industry and on the national and regional pattern of industrial development.

The United States, however, still finds the Canadian policies particularly troublesome, as they are seen as undercutting current US efforts to persuade other countries, especially in the developing world, to move away from such measures. Furthermore, they increase

pressures for the United States to adopt similar policies, to the detriment of the world trading and economic system as a whole, It is, indeed, the case that these Canadian policies played a part in strengthening the pressure for US legislation on "reciprocity" as well as the Administration's interest in bringing host country policies toward inward direct investment under the GATT, as discussed in the next chapter.

In January 1982, the United States raised the question of the imposition of trade conditions on investment as a complaint under Articles XXII and XXIII of the GATT. It is the first time that an issue of this kind has been brought to the GATT[10].

INDUSTRIALISED/DEVELOPING COUNTRIES

A debate persists within the GATT activities in Geneva between the industrialised and developing countries. This generally takes place in the Trade and Development Committee, a long standing body with a general remit as a forum for discussing all matters arising from the GATT, or from world trade matters, that are of interest to the developing countries. This Committee maintains a continuous review of implementation of Part IV of the GATT (the special articles dealing with the trade of developing countries) and since 1970 also of the "enabling clause" which was part of the Tokyo Round package. Although its powers have increased somewhat since 1980, the Committee cannot help being largely concerned with the grievances brought by the developing countries. These often include concern over what has been described as "the arbitrary and discriminatory" manner in which many developing countries consider certain donor countries were operating General Schemes of Preferences, by excluding some products on the grounds of the exporter having "graduated" to a more developed status. The complaint has been rejected by the industrialised countries.

So far as can be ascertained, no formal discussions have taken place in the GATT on the important issue of graduation. However, the question of treatment of exports from countries which have moved quite far up the scale of industrialisation, and which seem to be able to trade in the world on a competitive basis, is clearly of

---

10 The C.D. Howe Institute published, in 1981, *Trade Policy in the 1980s: An Agenda for Canadian/US Relations,* by Rodney De C. Grey.

increasing importance; and this leads directly to the underlying question of definition of a "developing" country.

So long as the share in world trade of countries other than those traditionally regarded as "developed" or "industrialised" was very small, the extent to which they conformed with the same rules of international trade was not very important. Equally, when the priviliges or immunities attached to the status of "developing" were shadowy and insubstantial, the same applied. However, both these conditions have now been changed. The "special and differential" provisions introduced into most of the Tokyo Round codes do, in fact, provide the status of "developing" with tangible benefits, and some countries so assisted, notably the NICs, have certainly been able to achieve a sizeable role in world exports in a limited number of products. It begins to seem very unfair, especially to industries in industrialised countries who have to face this competition, that the countries from which it comes should remain virtually free from obligation as regards their own tariff structures, or in relation to many others of the rules of the international system.

The countries concerned, on the other hand, see the other side of the picture, one in which they are treated as second-class members of the international trading community. In past tariff negotiations they have not had sufficient bargaining power to secure favourable treatment for products in which they have had special interest. They have found many products—especially agricultural products—still subject to quantitative restrictions in foreign markets, or being subsidised in ways which inhibited them from competing. And increasingly, in those areas of production where they have begun to become competitive, they see restrictions against their exports which are not only limitative, but often discriminatory. As they see it, the industrialised countries close ranks against the threat from newcomers, and do their best to resist the structural changes in the international division of labour which should in fact be resulting from the normal operation of the GATT. The leading case in this process is the continued insistence on refusing to allow the normal disciplines of international trade to operate in the textile industry.

The resolution of these issues is, of course, bound up with the major piece of unfinished business of the Tokyo Round—the discussion of emergency safeguard measures—and it is related also to the general issue of "structural adjustment", and therefore to the whole question of subsidies and other means of indirect protection of domestic industries.

Certainly no very easy answer is to be found on "graduation". The best that the OECD countries could do on this subject in their 1982 Ministerial meeting was to note the "growing role of developing countries in international trade and investment" and to agree "that it would be important to facilitate the fuller participation of these countries in the open and multilateral trading system, with its shared rights and responsibilities, in order to provide a sound basis for their progressive integration into the world market economy."

However, the OECD Ministers went on to say that they foresaw a need to improve arrangements for examining and resolving international economic problems of special relevance to developing countries, and to offer to discuss with them "how this process can be advanced in the appropriate international fora" (by which is presumably meant the GATT, as far as trade matters are concerned).

A continuing and troublesome problem certainly exists. But it may perhaps be supposed that the atmosphere in Geneva is to some extent moving away from the previous insistence on "special and differential" treatment towards realisation, by some developing countries, that it may be more important for them to try to secure themselves against imposition of restrictions. There may, therefore, perhaps be some room for advance on both sides—some reduction in protection and fuller observance of GATT rules by advanced developing countries, and greater security of access to market, without recourse to restriction, in the industrialised countries.

How far this might go in the short term is still very uncertain. But it seems probable, in the present atmosphere, that some evolutionary development along these lines might be more promising than a formal assault on the definition of a "developing country".

V The GATT Ministerial Meeting: November 1982

In the preceding sections, the analysis of developments since the Tokyo Round, the actions of governments, and the issues arising between countries and groups of countries, has given a general indication of the international commercial policy issues which are currently on the table. In this analysis, we have referred to most, though not quite all, of the topics which are likely to be discussed at the GATT Ministerial Meeting to be held in Geneva in November 1982, and have dealt with some of them fairly fully. Not all the matters mentioned will necessarily appear on the agenda of that meeting, but all of them are relevant to the current atmosphere surrounding international trade policy. Whether or not they are actually on the table for discussion, they will certainly be part of the background of the meeting's debates, and will influence its outcome.

We have now to draw together the threads of this analysis, and try to put together which items are likely to appear on the agenda, and what are likely to be the attitudes taken by the main participants. In making these assessments, we can draw on a fair amount of US material about what the Administration would like to see discussed[11]. The European Commission have also communicated to the Council of Ministers of the Community their general recommendations on many of the matters at issue[12]. At this time of writing, however, there is very little indication of the Japanese views likely to be taken.

PERCEPTIONS OF PURPOSE

On at least the crucial importance of the meeting, however, the United States and the European Community are agreed, and they speak in virtually the same words as each other—and it happens, as the Director General of the GATT. In his Hamburg speech, Mr. Dunkel said:

"The tendency towards bilateralism and sectoralism in trade policy is the greatest present danger both politically and

---

11 See Appendix IV for a full statement of US views in testimony from Mr. William Brock, US Special Trade Representative to the Trade Subcommittee of the House of Representatives and House Ways and Means Committee, October 28th and 29th 1981. More recent statements (eg, Mr. Brock's statement to the Subcommittee for International Trade, Senate Finance Committee March 1st 1982) are similar, but less detailed.

12 This is reproduced in Appendix II.

economically to order and prosperity in the world economy. In political terms, it must undermine the credibility of those in industrialised countries who champion the open trading system and commend it to the developing world. More profoundly, it endangers the very possibility of maintaining the international economic co-operation which has made possible the progress of the last 30 years."[13]

An official US background statement on US goals at the Versailles Summit in June 1982 put it this way:

"Worldwide recession and high unemployment in many countries are bringing the outcry for trade restrictions to a high level of intensity. But US State Department officials argue that this makes it even more important to reaffirm the principle that the long term direction should be towards free trade, and to underscore the danger that giving in to protectionist demands would do further damage to the world economy—as it did in the 1930's."[14]

Finally, Sir Roy Denman, then Director General for External Relations in the European Commission, in his speech at Houston in May 1982 said:

"All this means not only a dangerously stagnant situation in relation to world trade, but protectionist pressures and strains— in all the major trading countries of the world—on the social fabric which imperil the open world trading system on which the prosperity of the free world has been built since the war . . . A failure at the end of the year to agree on major points . . . could mark the beginning of reversion to the protectionism— with its political consequences—of the 1930's."[15]

Given this remarkable degree of consensus about the nature and extent of the dangers in the present situation and trends, it might have been supposed that both the Community and the United States would be anxious to take steps to try to cool the situation, and to move towards more conciliatory attitudes, both towards each other, and towards Japan and other countries also. If anything,

---

13 See Appendix I

14 *US Goals at the Versailles Summit,* issued by the US International Communications Agency, May 19th 1982.

15 Denman, op. cit.

however—at any rate up to the time when this is written, in September 1982—the reverse is happening, and causes of conflict are piling up. The United States action on steel; the Community's complaint on DISC; the Community's pursuit of its general complaining against Japan; a hardening of attitudes, especially perhaps by the United States, on some of the issues in which the developing countries are interested—all these begin to cast a shadow of doubt over both the Ministerial Meeting and the future well being of international trade. Indeed, the European Commission, in communicating to the Council of Ministers its "General Policy Orientation" for the GATT Meeting, refers with foreboding to the possibility that "certain trends which appear to put into question the international trading rules agreed on in the GATT may be confirmed", and that if this happens, it would change inevitably the context in which the meeting takes place.

However, in spite of these background shadows, active work, on a co-operative basis, has been making progress in Geneva in preparing the ground for the Ministerial Meeting, and it is possible to compile a reasonable picture of what is likely to be the content of the discussion, with some indication of the probable attitudes of the principal participants on most of the issues—always supposing that it does not founder on the rocks of current dissensions.

THE WORK OF THE MEETING

The meeting is seen as undertaking three tasks. First, it would formulate a "Declaration"—a common re-assertion of faith in and adherence to the GATT and the open trading system, and an attempt to agree on an assessment of the problems facing the system. Second, there would be an attempt to reach decisions on some issues, if possible on substance, or at least on some time scale for decisions of substance. Thirdly, there would be discussion towards agreement on a programme of work on a variety of issues, which one or a few member countries would like to be examined in detail, perhaps to discover what, if any, GATT action might be possible, perhaps in order to establish that such action was not feasible or not appropriate.

Whether or not this all adds up to a "Round" of negotiations is not a very important question. US spokesmen have sometimes spoken of the November meeting as being the starting point which would lead to a new Round, while at other times avoiding such language. The Community, firmly, does not regard a new major Round of trade negotiations as a "practicable" outcome, but does not rule out the possibility of limited *ad hoc* understandings, or the establishment of a programme of discussions on which progress would be made over a period of years. On this general approach, there may not be very great differences between the United States and Community positions, though—as frequently in the past—the former will probably want to be seen to be pursuing all the objectives in sight with vigour and zeal, while the Community will be on the side of prudent deliberation. And there will certainly be very substantial differences between them on many issues of detail, even about the content of a work-programme. The further the topic, or the drafting, moves from the realms of generalisation, the more acute these differences will become.

The Declaration

The high-sounding "declaration" in general terms would, no doubt, present little difficulty. But, as we have seen, there have been many such declarations in the very recent past; and what comes out of Geneva must say something different from what came from the Versailles summit and the Paris OECD Ministerial Meeting if it is to carry any conviction. At the least it would require a frank acknowledgment from the major governments that many of the policies they have pursued in the past and many that they are still pursuing—and in most countries the general direction of much of their policy—are the very causes of the dangers which face the open trading system. The dangers are real; but to avert them requires more than assertions of faith. It needs successful actions, which have to be taken especially by the major countries, to reverse both the persistent economic recession and the trend of attitudes in trade policy.

There is not very much so far to suggest that either the Community or the United States is seriously considering the full implications for their domestic policies of their diagnosis of the dangers on the international trade front. Each of them is, of course, aware of the sins of the other. If, therefore, the drafting process seriously attempts to give the Declaration a broad political sweep, we may expect that some of the conflicts described above will be brought into the debate.

In that case, we may see the Community and the United States each trying to introduce the grievances they have against each other and against Japan. On the macro-economic issues, there may be all too easy agreement that what is required is a resumption of economic growth, because slow growth retards trade and makes more difficult the problems of structural adjustment. But the Community may try to refer to what it sees as the harmful results of high American interest rates and other aspects of US economic policy, as well as other political trade issues—such as the unsettling effects of possible US legislation on "reciprocity", the difficulties resulting from trade embargoes, and the harassment aspects of US trade legislation. In its turn, the United States would point to the long standing disturbance to world patterns of trade and the economies of many countries, which it sees as resulting from Community policies, in particular the Common Agricultural Policy, massive state subsidisation of industries, and in general, intervention by government in detailed business decisions.

If, indeed, these matters were to be examined openly, and each side were to recognise that its own policies contributed to the problem and needed serious reappraisal, a Declaration might begin to have something more than merely ritual significance.

Matters for "Decision"

This Section (and the next) will be based on the headings which seem to have emerged from the preliminary discussions which have been taking place in Geneva over recent months, supplemented by what can be deduced from other sources, chiefly US and the Community; so far as possible, the likely views of the participants are noted under each heading.

Developing Countries. We have already discussed (pages 39-41) the main issues between the industrialised and the developing countries. The developing countries will, no doubt, wish to see their concerns prominently on the agenda, which is not likely to be resisted. The central issue continues to be "special and differential treatment"; but as we have indicated, this will not necessarily be pushed to extremes.

The general approaches to the developing countries of the Europeans and Americans (and probably of the Japanese also) are not significantly different in intention and effect, though their presentation may differ in emphasis and style. The present US tendency is to be unequivocally downright, indeed somewhat aggressive, in resisting claims which the United States does not accept; this has led to its receiving rather more obloquy than has sometimes been justified. The Community uses rather more shaded and equivocal language. The Commission has now set out fairly clearly the line which it proposes the Community should adopt. This says, in effect, that there is not much room, at any rate in the short term, for further reductions of tariffs or other barriers against developing country exports, over and above the Tokyo Round concessions. In particular, "non-reciprocity" cannot continue to be applicable to *all* developing countries. The more advanced, specifically the NICs, should increasingly accept commitments and responsibilities closer to those of the developed countries; the present assumption of substantial exemption from obligations has to be challenged, and to be applied more selectively. The emphasis of special treatment must be shifted from applicability to all developing countries towards concentrating on the less advanced (including the Community's associated countries, most of whom are in this category). One line of progress would be for the more advanced to open their own markets more freely to other developing countries, and especially the least developed. (The Commission does not, however, try to specify what products Chad, say, might be able to sell to Brazil or South Korea. Nor does it appear aware that Hong Kong has a market open to the whole world, without tariffs or other restrictions of any kind—a frequent example of myopia in this area of discussion).

Whether this approach (which may be expected to be, in general, acceptable also to the United States and most other industrialised countries) will in fact lead to agreed "decisions" remains to be seen. What it does mean, in any case, is that relations between industrialised and developing countries will almost certainly continue to move in a somewhat piecemeal and pragmatic way, which will avoid a frontal assault on the concept of graduation and the question of definition of a "developing" country. It will try to produce the result of having rules without formulating them. This may perhaps work in the short term, and it may well be the only practicable way to proceed. However, it will continue to leave the issues unsettled and the overall situation distinctly untidy, with the ever-present threat of more troublesome confrontations in other international fora—the UNCTAD and the United Nations.

Safeguards. The question of a new formulation for the GATT "Safeguard" clause (Article XIX) was perhaps the chief piece of unfinished business of the Tokyo Round. It is also one in which the developing countries have a substantial interest.

The safeguard clause is, so to speak, the GATT's last resort mechanism for emergency action on imports of particular products. It enables countries to impose restrictions on imports to the extent and for such time as may be necessary to prevent or remedy serious injury, or the threat of such injury, to domestic producers. It also provides various procedures for retaliatory measures in some circumstances, or for compensatory concessions. For a variety of reasons, the GATT Article as it stands has not proved a satisfactory basis. One principal reason for this has been its implication that if it is invoked, any restrictions imposed should be non-discriminatory among all the sources of imports, whereas those who have wished to invoke it have usually wanted to restrict supplies from particular sources which they regard as "responsible" for the damage or threat. As a result, Article XIX has been widely disregarded, but countries have either taken unilateral action on imports, or have secured "voluntary" export controls by the troublesome exporter, or the government of the exporting country.

It is generally accepted that the existing situation is very unsatisfactory, and does damage to the whole fabric of the international trade rules. The problem, which the Tokyo Round discussions failed to solve, is to find an agreement which adequately balances two undesirable extremes. On the one hand lies the danger of making it so easy and legitimate for importing countries to resort to safeguard measures that these become the normal and natural response to any increase in foreign competition—an approach that simply facilitates and sanctifies protectionism. On the other hand is the risk of making safeguards so difficult to employ and hedging them with such a degree of surveillance and conditioning that importing countries will again simply disregard the rules when they feel that they cannot, or do not wish to, withstand domestic pressures for protection.

It is not easy to recognise any general change in world conditions which would make this problem simpler to solve now than in 1979. However, the European Commission seems to suggest that a new approach might now be possible. This is based on the proposition that since a wide range of measures is already being applied on a "selective" basis (ie. the basis for which the Community has always argued), there may be greater readiness to reach some compromise. Perhaps selectivity would not be ruled out *a priori* (in circumstances where this might be less restrictive for world trade) in return for a greater degree of transparency, and some surveillance of the kind of measures outside the scope of Article XIX which have been commonly used.

The United States has not yet made clear how far it would be prepared to go toward selectivity. But some aspects of its recent policies might be read as indicating a greater readiness to go at least some way than it did during the Tokyo Round.

Since it is the active exporters who are the potential victims of greater selectivity in any new rules that might emerge, the developing countries, especially the NICs as well as Japan, might feel that almost any arrangement of this kind is likely to condone and encourage protectionism rather than to inhibit it.

Although *Agriculture* has seemed to be less prominent on the US priority list for urgent examination than previously, many countries—including Australia and New Zealand—will want to see it fully discussed by Ministers.

This will, of course, mean that the acute differences of view between the United States and the Community (discussed on pages 28-32) will be brought into the argument. The European Commission considers it quite unrealistic to try to apply the normal GATT rules to agriculture; indeed it argues that this was never the intention of the GATT from the beginning. It accepts the general desirability of working towards an open multilateral trading system for agriculture as for other sectors, but stresses that in this objective all forms of direct and indirect protection and support, as well as the political and economic conditions underlying them require negotiation.

How vigorously the United States will contest this is uncertain. In the present state of tension the Community would no doubt be prepared to challenge the US general waiver, which since 1952 has allowed the United States a considerable measure of latitude in its own agricultural policies.

What might perhaps emerge from the Ministerial Meeting is some general additional commitment to "transparency" for the agricultural policies of all countries, and some further modest institutional development—perhaps by establishing an Agricultural Committee which would formalise the existing informal arrangements of the Group of 18 for regular discussion of agricultural matters.

General Tariff and Non-Tariff Measures. Under this heading we may expect to see discussed—in general terms but not in detail—the various matters arising out of the Geneva work in the aftermath of the Tokyo Round which were described in Chapter III above (pages 14-21). In general, these should not be contentious, and the Meeting should be able to achieve a sufficient consensus on most of them to produce agreement on setting out a continuing work programme.

On tariffs, it should be possible to agree in principle the harmonised nomenclature system, and on the conduct of negotiations about its consequences. There may be a little more difficulty about the points at issue between industrialised and developing countries.

On non-tariff measures, the various Tokyo Round Agreements (the "Codes") have, for the most part, their own built-in provisions for periodic review, and in some cases for new negotiations on specific issues (eg. the extension of the list of entities covered by the Code on Government Procurement). In line with the rationale of the Ministerial Meeting, however, there should doubtless be a general political appraisal of the operation, effectiveness, and coverage of the Codes, and of the extent to which their implementation and results have achieved what was hoped for them.

One Code in particular may provide an exception to the general non-contentiousness of this area of the agenda, that on Subsidies and Countervailing. The debate, here again chiefly between the United States and the Community, will centre not so much on substance as on the way in which the disputes settlement procedures are being used and are working.

Disputes Settlement. A number of countries, including particularly Canada, seem to be taking the view that the disputes settlement procedures of both the GATT itself and under the Tokyo Round Codes, are not working satisfactorily, and that the credibility of the whole system may be at risk unless there is an improvement.

It is not altogether clear what specific criticism is made of the procedures, nor how exactly it is thought that they should be remedied. However, there can be little doubt that the Geneva process for dealing with disputes is both slow and cumbersome, and that it may also often be ineffectual, since there is no machinery of enforcement except through authorised retaliation.

The United States has taken no public stand on this issue; but as we have noted, it has, over the period since the end of the Tokyo Round, embarked on a much more zealous and persistent use of the complaints mechanism. The European Community has seen this as in itself a source of annoyance. Indeed, the European Commission sees as the very causes of the difficulties the emphasis given to systematic and almost automatic use of the procedures, and what it calls the unrealistic expectation that they can solve difficulties in a semi-juridical way, by giving binding rulings, or by producing results which could not be achieved in the negotiations.

We may therefore see a major clash of positions if disputes-settlement procedures become an important focus of the Meeting. In fact, this topic does in itself encapsulate many of the causes of tension between the major participants.

It would be unfortunate if the debate on this subject did in the event develop on those lines. Well informed observers and well-wishers of the GATT system take the view that an improved and better functioning system in this area offers the most useful path for advance in the difficult circumstances in which world trade is likely to be conducted over the next few years. They see the consequences of the inter-relationship between domestic policies and international trade (as discussed in Chapter III above in pages 23-25) as implying that a much greater range of policies which have previously been thought of as primarily, if not entirely, matters of domestic concern, will increasingly come to be regarded as appropriate subjects for international concern. (Domestic subsidies are, of course, one of the leading and most obvious cases). It will, however, be quite impossible to formulate even general rules for this immense and shifting range of policies. The only possible way to accommodate this situation would be in a well-operated and adequate system covering not only disputes but also notification, surveillance, consultation and conciliation. Over time, international co-operation in such a system could build up a corpus of common views on acceptable and reasonable patterns of conduct and policies. It seems improbable however, that either the United States or the Community is disposed to launch ideas of this kind, at any rate in the 1982 Ministerial Meeting.

Matters for Future Examination, and Possible Future Extensions of the GATT

For the most part, what has been discussed in the preceding section will provide the continuing programme of work, and official discussion among officials of contracting parties, at the GATT over the next few years. However, largely as the result of US efforts and of initiatives, three further substantial topics which have so far been of only marginal significance for the GATT are likely to be on the Ministerial Meeting Agenda. These are trade in services, host country regulations on inward investment that may effect trade ("trade-related investment issues" in the jargon phrase) and trade in high-technology products (which is, of course, subject to existing GATT rules, but where some special considerations may be thought to arise). There can clearly be no "decisions" on these three topics by Ministers in November. But they might be referred for study, in Geneva and in capitals, to see whether, and if so how, it would be feasible and appropriate to bring them within the scope of the GATT.

Services. The service industries and international trade in services have become progressively more important in the economies of the industrialised countries. In the United States about 70% of all employment is in this sector, which produces about 65% of the GNP. The figure for the other major countries are of the same order. Not all services of course, are traded internationally; but they account for about 25% of total exports by OECD countries (35% to 40% for some countries such as the United States and the United Kingdom). With minor and historically accidental exceptions (notably cinematograph film distribution and exhibition), the GATT did not concern itself with the substantial volume of such trade, and there has so far been no significant effort to provide any general framework of international rules for its conduct. This gap in the GATT's coverage has become the subject of increasing attention, mainly on US initiative (but with considerable interest from the service industries in a number of countries, and from the International Chamber of Commerce).

On the international scene, work continues to be done, in the OECD. But if there is to be an international framework of rules, it would almost certainly be best focussed in the GATT. However, there are formidable conceptual and practical problems to be examined before it can be concluded that such a framework is even feasible, let alone what it might contain.

The United States, will of course, actively promote the study of the subject in the GATT. The European Community has been more hesitant, and more inclined to emphasise the difficulties. One of these may be that the developing countries, some of which are trying to build up service industries of their own—banking, insurance, shipping—under rather restrictive regimes, may be reluctant to accept the promulgation of GATT-type rules in this field. The Community now, however, seems unlikely to oppose a programme of study, if it is confined at this stage to providing the material on which to assess whether and how GATT disciplines might be applied.

Trade-Related Investment Issues. The subject of "performance requirements" exchanged for permission to foreign firms to undertake or expand investment in a "host" country has been referred to above (pages 37-39) as a main cause of friction between the United States and Canada. The United States believes, however, that to a greater or lesser extent, some form of action of this kind is practised by the governments of most of its trading partners. The requirements may include commitments by investing firms to export specific quantities, to incorporate specified amounts of local components, or to offset the firm's imports by at least a corresponding amount of exports. Much American opinion regards such action as wholly protectionist in character

At the same time, however, there is powerful support in Congress and among the labour unions for US legislation to impose performance requirements on foreign investors in the United States. The United States Government has shown its dislike for these moves, which weaken its own ability to press the matter in the GATT.

Here, again, the European Community, after some initial hesitation, now seems disposed to see itself as having an interest in supporting the US proposal. The Community might indeed agree to study the possibility of establishing an inventory of investment regulations that may distort trade and then formulating rules to be applied. It is not at all certain, however, that all other countries will be equally agreeable to such a development, though there is unlikely to be determined opposition to studies on a noncommital basis.

Trade in High-Technology Products. It is not altogether clear what the United States (supported to some extent by Japan) intends, or hopes, should emerge from this last of its three initiatives, since high-technology products are certainly as much subject to the GATT as any other manufactured goods. The objective could be to work out some form of free-trade agreement like that on civil aircraft, but this seems a somewhat forlorn hope. On the other hand, it may be that a number of countries are building up excessive protection, through policies of subsidisation and preferential purchasing, for domestic industries (the "industries of the future"), and that this will call for special international examination.

Whatever the motive, the outcome in November 1982 can hardly do more than authorise further study in the most general terms and on a very guarded and non-committal basis.

VI Conclusion

The preceding chapters have used the Ministerial Meeting of GATT, to be held in November 1982, as the peg on which to hang a discussion which does in fact cover the matters discussed in the broader title—"Trade Issues in the Mid-1980's." In addition, the occasion has been taken to continue the record of trade policy developments which was begun in the two previous Reports in the series. Taken together, the three Reports aim to provide a continuous account of these developments since the beginning of the Tokyo Round—that is from the Ministerial Meeting of September 1973 to its successor in November 1982, and to the tasks and problems beyond.

Both of the preceding Reports ended with the hope that the negotiations then in progress—the Tokyo Round—would contribute to a restoration of growth in international trade, and an improvement in international trading conditions; but into each a note of doubt intruded. In February 1974, I wrote:

> "In the present state of the world, and of international economic and political relations, it would be unrealistic and utopian to suppose that the GATT negotiations will, in the short term, have very much more than marginal effects on the scale and pattern of world trade, or on the conduct of national policies. But it would surely be too great a counsel of despair to believe that the great trading powers of the world will not find, through these negotiations, the way to preserve and to restore the will and the means for continuing international co-operation and progress."

And in March 1978:

> "In the last analysis, international relations depend on what governments actually do, not on the formal rules which purport to govern their conduct. The General Agreement on Tariffs and Trade was the same Agreement in the 1970's as in the 1950's. What had changed was the degree of willingness of Governments to abide by the principles which had seemed to have become the generally accepted norms of international practice, and which they still held out to be the basis on which their policies were founded . . . The important thing is to maintain sufficient confidence in the basic will of governments to reverse their current drift into economic nationalism."

If the 1978 conclusion was more pessimistic than that of 1974, it is difficult, in July 1982, to find much new ground for optimism.

What one can say, however, is that in spite of everything the GATT does survive still, and that governments do still feel it necessary to re-assert their adherence to it. If the present discontents can be surmounted, the 1982 Ministerial Meeting can even now make its contribution to a reversal of the drift into bitter trade war between the major trading powers, with the consequences that would bring for all the countries of the world. But it will be the actions and policies of Governments over the next years which will decide this outcome, not the minutiae of the communiqué from Geneva at the end of the 38th Session (held at Ministerial level) of the Contracting Parties to the GATT.

Address by Mr. Arthur Dunkel, Director-General, GATT, at "Ostasiatisches Liebesmahl", Hamburg, 5 March 1982.

I regard it as a great honour to have been invited to speak to you tonight, knowing as I do the long line of distinguished men who have addressed the Ostasiatisches Liebesmahl in years gone by. For the same reason, it is a daunting challenge, too, but I know I start with the advantage of an audience predisposed in favour of the message that must be carried by the Director-General of the GATT. In this city, with the great Hanseatic tradition of openness to the world, and particularly to an audience committed to trading with Asia, there is little need to preach the gospel of free trade. There may be need, however, for the friends of the open trade system to recognise that passive support is no longer enough if the system is to be preserved.

In preparing this speech I naturally called to mind my own recent experience of the countries of Asia. In the last 14 months I have visited India, Pakistan, Hong Kong and all the countries of ASEAN in my capacity as Director-General of GATT. In all of these countries I occasionally felt as if I were there on false pretences—as if I should have presented a card indicating that I was ex officio Chairman of the GATT committee in charge of the Multifibre Arrangement: for in all of them the MFA seems better known than the GATT.

That businessmen and politicians in Asia consider GATT's activities primarily from the viewpoint of textiles and clothing is understandable. After all, textiles and clothing account for 10% of their total exports, and 20% of their exports of manufactures. But it is very worrying, on several accounts.

I believe that failure to renew the MFA in December would have entailed disruption and uncertainty going far beyond the textile sector—that there was in fact no sensible alternative. But we have to recognise that the MFA is a negotiated derogation from the basic law of international trade. It allows the main principles of the GATT to be ignored in a crucially important sector of world trade. For countries which are critically dependent on textiles, this is bound to call in question the sincerity of those in the West who so often, and so eloquently, proclaim their dedication to the principles of liberal trade.

It is often said, of course, that textiles is an unfortunate, unavoidable but unique exception from the rules, and I would not have made so much of it tonight but for the fact that, in recent years, one sector after another—steel, shipbuilding, synthetic fibres, automobiles, not to mention agriculture, where intervention has become institutionalised—has been subjected to special arrangements with protectionist effects. By this I mean the so-called self-restraint and orderly marketing agreements. These sectoral deals differ from the MFA in being essentially bilateral and wholly outside the rule of law. So far they have involved mainly the industrialised countries, though some developing countries of Asia are being drawn into them. These arrangements resemble the MFA in being presented as regrettable temporary expedients, necessitated by short-term pressures or crises. But every time a government cedes to such pressure it makes it more difficult for itself and for other governments to resist the next demand, and more likely that new demands will be made.

The tendency towards bilateralism and sectoralism in trade policy is the greatest present danger both politically and economically to order and prosperity in the world economy. In political terms, it must undermine the credibility of those in industrialised countries who champion the open trading system and commend it to the developing world. More profoundly, it endangers the very possibility of maintaining the international economic co-operation which has made possible the progress of the last 30 years: for the co-operation can only be based on multilateralism and obedience to general rules.

When commercial policy is conducted on a sectoral basis, the interaction between industrial lobbies and national administrations makes an eventual return to liberal trading extremely difficult. To take away a privileged position is always more difficult than to refuse it in the first place. It is more likely, as bureaucrats identify with the interests of "their" industries, that restrictions will be tightened. We cannot perhaps blame the textile manufacturers of the industrialised world for losing sight of the fact that the overall trade deficit of the industrialised countries in textiles and clothing is offset, as to about 80%, by their exports of dyes, synthetic fibres and textile machinery to the developing world. But governments can be blamed if they fail to see it: their prime function is to appreciate the global, not sectional, interests of their own countries and, if possible, of the world.

A foreign trade policy has to consider national trade needs globally. It operates by fairly simple rules of general application. Trade policy in this sense is being progressively supplanted by a series of discrete sectoral trade policies which, being laboriously negotiated first between the government and each industry lobby, and then between the government and each exporting country, do not lend themselves to coordination. As such deals proliferate, coherent policy-making becomes impossible. Economic efficiency is lost at every stage, for the essential purpose of these arrangements is to frustrate the market in its function of allocating resources efficiently. They represent—and I am sure their authors know it—a collapse of confidence in the ability of our economies to adjust to competitive pressures and in the ability of governments to co-operate for the common good. They are in fact an admission of failure, for, surely,none of the policy-makers of the major developed countries believes that protectionist policies can do anything but harm. But the most pernicious aspect of sectoralism is perhaps that even the governments which practise it seem able to disguise from themselves its essentially protectionist character.

An equally dangerous distortion of competitive conditions, which is also spreading rapidly, is the use of subsidies, both domestically and in export markets. The fact that in all Western economies subsidies have risen sharply in relation to GNP over the last 10 or 15 years, and that they are increasingly given *in addition* to protection, is a logical consequence of the sectoral approach—a consequence, let me say, which is logical and absurd at the same time. In the highly trade-intensive Western economies, most industries export even though they also have to compete with imports in their domestic markets. In the present circumstances, a subsidy or increased protection against imports is seldom sufficient to *improve* their profitability; usually it only restores these industries' competitiveness on the domestic market by validating previous increases in their production costs relative to the costs of their foreign competitors. Without an additional subsidy, industries in this situation could not maintain their shares in export. In passing, I should say that the growth of competition through export subsidies poses a special problem for developing countries, which cannot afford to join that game, but cannot afford either to allow the terms of competition to be thus turned against them. And so, as each country protects its national industry domestically, all of them together are, by subsidies, artifically intensifying the competition of these industries in the export market—which, of course, consists of each other's domestic markets, the same markets all are trying to protect.

We can of course understand the tensions and the commercial and industrial conflicts that are growing among the industrialised nations. Trade is slowing down, unemployment grows, inflation is high, and everybody is looking for somebody to blame. Every government has a need to find scapegoats when the effects of its policies turn out not to be the ones it has expected and announced. Thus, the problem of competition with Japan has begun to assume the proportions of a crisis, though in reality it is only a symptom of the more general problem—and Japan is only the forerunner of a series of highly efficient newcomers on world markets for manufacturers. The West appears to be mesmerised by the spectacular productivity of Japanese industry—but the far-sighted Japanese are already worrying about Korea, India and, in 10 years perhaps, China.

I know that exporting to Japan poses special problems. The Japanese Government itself has recognised that there are things it should do to facilitate the entry of foreign goods, and has begun to implement them. This is to be welcomed, but is not a panacea: we must not forget the important truth which Ludwig Erhard preached in the 1950s, that an economy becomes more, not less, efficient as it opens itself up to imports.

A better functioning of the international monetary system, which would enable Japanese society, through a higher exchange rate, to reap the benefits of its efficiency in the form of cheaper imports, would greatly reduce these tensions. But in my view the only permanent solution to the so-called "Japanese problem" is for the Western economies to raise their productivity to Japanese levels, to accept the challenge. It is possible to exclude more efficient producers from one's domestic market, at great political and economic cost; but the corollary is acceptance of defeat in third markets.

Finally we have to consider the effects on the international order of the sectorialisation of commercial policy. A particular consequence is that the necessary balance between the industrial and the financial side of the economy can no longer be maintained. Countries with heavy foreign debt must be able to export if they are to service their debt without cutting back imports. In the years following the 1973-1974 oil crisis, exports from industrial to developing countries were the most rapidly expanding flow of international trade, sustaining the level of economic activity in the industrialised countries. The expansion was possible because, in those years, the developing countries were able to borrow from the highly liquid international capital market. The level of foreign debt is now very high, and so are real interest rates. The indebtedness can be sustained only by a continuing, if not accelerated, expansion of trade. But in 1980 and 1981, the growth of trade has been slowing down.

Thus all countries are hit when the international trade system ceases to function satisfactorily. Those introducing the restrictions suffer most severely, for two reasons. Protection and subsidies distort their industrial structure away from that which would be required for more rapid industrial growth. Equally if not more important, protection also threatens the soundness of their financial institutions. The capacity of international trade to contribute to the recovery of industrial economies is thus lost.

I may perhaps have stated the case too bluntly. I know that in times as difficult as these there are always persuasive arguments for deviations from the general rules, and I recognise that even in normal times full observance of them is not to be expected. The GATT itself contains "escape clauses", and has a record of waivers and exceptions both negotiated and otherwise. But what is disturbing in the present situation is the growing dimension of the "grey area" in which restrictions are imposed without legal sanction, the feeling that we are confronted with a gradual erosion that is even more difficult to deal with than an open crisis. Even governments themselves are beginning openly to doubt their capacity to stave off the crisis they fear coming. Thus we are told from the highest level that protectionism is no longer a possibility but a probability. Elsewhere the notion is gaining influential adherence that trade should be conducted on the basis of strict reciprocity—which in my view implies repudiation of existing international obligations, and of all the lessons of the past which have demonstrated that strict reciprocity is technically infeasible.

I am also frequently told that the rules of the GATT fulfilled perhaps their function in a given time but have since become obsolete, and are now ineffective in the face of contemporary problems. In response I usually point out that lately, the rules have not been given much chance to prove themselves. Solutions to the most important problems of international trade policy are largely being sought through ad hoc accommodations between small groups of countries outside GATT rules. So how can we *know* that the rules are ineffective? Whereupon these apparently well-meaning people explain to me that it has been necessary to take these apparently short-term but acute problems out of the GATT, in order to alleviate the strain on its poor, old and fragile rules.

Let us look at this attitude more closely. When people say the rules of the GATT have become ineffective, they are only saying that the rules are not being observed. Mutual accommodation is thought to be easier through private arrangements in which GATT commitments are politely ignored; and I admit such arrangements, viewed individually, may be easier in the short run, and for the short run only. But they create precedents, the relief granted to one industry is difficult to deny to another, and so after a while we are . . . well, we are where we are.

The critics of the rules are in effect saying that the rules ceased to be respected because they were "unrealistic", too strict, too demanding, to begin with. From which it seems to follow logically that looser, more permissive rules would be more faithfully followed—or more strictly observed—by the governments. Is it so difficult to see that this proposition is self-contradictory and empty, indeed stunningly trivial?

Allow me therefore a few remarks on the rôle of rules in international trade policy, a rôle which I conceive of as the rule of law in intergovernmental relations.

Discrimination in trade has been historically a main source of international conflict. The long period of peaceful prosperity between the Napoleonic wars and World War I was very largely based on the *système des traités*—commercial treaties which, though concluded bilaterally, formed a multilateral system, being interlinked by the most-favoured-clauses which constitutes the central commitment of each. After World War I it proved impossible to restore this system, we all know with what consequences. What GATT achieved after World War II was actually nothing revolutionary: it succeeded in restoring that older system. It innovated only in placing it on an explicitly multilateral basis, and in greatly increasing the number of countries participating in the multilateral treaty system.

Let me recall that in the 1920s the words "reciprocity" and "nondiscrimination" (or "unconditional most-favoured-nation pledge") denoted contradictions, mutually exclusive alternatives. The fact that in the GATT countries have been negotiating and contracting with each other on the basis of reciprocity *and* non-descrimination is due to their understanding that reciprocity is always a subjective notion which cannot be looked at in bilateral terms. It cannot be determined exactly; it can only be *agreed upon*, and such agreement is possible only among countries sharing a commitment to some higher principle which, in the case of GATT, has been, simply, the rule of law. This is what I meant by saying that strict reciprocity is technically not feasible as the sole basis for any one nation's commercial policy. One side alone cannot decide what reciprocity is.

Let me go further and say that international economic policy commitments, in the form of agreed rules, have far-reaching domestic effects, indeed effects so important that they are indispensable for domestic governance. They are the element which secures the ultimate co-ordination and mutual compatibility of the purely domestic economic policies. They form the basis from which the government can arbitrate and secure an equitable and efficient balance between the diverse domestic interests: producers *versus* consumers, export industries *versus* import-competing industries, between particular narrowly defined industries. Last but not least, only a firm commitment to international rules makes possible the all-important reconciliation, which I have already alluded to, of the necessary balance on the production side and on the financial side of the national economy.

In all these ways the commitment to international rules defines and fixes the permanent national interest in economic matters—which, I repeat, is an indispensable function in a democratic system providing for an orderly change of political governments at relatively frequent intervals.

It is thus nothing but intellectual laziness to consider these international disciplines to be an undue constraint on governments, something of a concession from national interest to international comity. This amounts to saying that a government free from external constraints would be better or more completely able to secure all the interests of its nation. But this is about as deep and useful an insight as saying that in a world in which there was no scarcity of goods we would all be better off. Another way of explaining the current political and economic malaise is to say that it stems from an unwillingness to think carefully about the difficult but important concept of national interest.

It seems appropriate here to ask if the system of law which governments have laid down in the GATT no longer in their judgement corresponds to the national interests of their countries, or whether the problem is that these countries are no longer willing to make the continuous adjustments which the system demands.

It will be no surprise to you, in the light of what I have said already, that I believe the second explanation is the true one. I am still convinced that it is in the national interest of every trading nation to abide by the rules, which were accepted as valid for good times and bad, and to frame their internal policies accordingly. One of the major benefits of international disciplines is that they offer equal opportunities and require comparable sacrifices from all the countries involved in international competition. Those who believe in the open trading system must recognise and accept the need to correct those rigidities in their economic and social systems which obstruct the process of continuing adjustment on which economic growth depends. Once decision-makers in the economy are convinced that governments are resolved to follow this line, one may hope that the present crisis of confidence would be overcome and the recovery might begin. I know that this is easier said than done, and that it calls for effort and sacrifice, but I see no alternative

Conclusion

Our present problems—unemployment, inflation, stagnating growth and stagnating trade—make strict adherence to international rules especially difficult. But can we wait for the heavy weather to blow away before we reaffirm the rules? Surely not, for if we waited we would be saying that not only the GATT system but rule of law as such, democratic constitutionalism, are not only fair-weather ideas.

Our economists explain the economic difficulties I have mentioned in terms of uncertainty—uncertainty which the rules were designed to minimise, did successfully minimise for more than 20 years, and which then returned and grew as exceptions from the rules grew more common. I do not have to expand on the consequences. You know better than I what it is to make long-term contracts and commitments in a situation where uncertainty has been enhanced because rules have ceased to be reliable.

Fortunately, there are signs that an increasing number of governments are concerned about the trend of events, and about the danger to the multilateral system which its constitution would pose. It is not simply that bilateral solutions are seen to be unstable, or that ad hoc deals in one sector are found to exacerbate difficulties in another. The habit of international co-operation, based on respect for general rules of economic behaviour, which has underpinned the enormous material progress of the post-war era, is seen to be threatened. Governments which badly need each other's understanding and support are dragged into dangerous disputes over sectional interests which are themselves inimical to the national welfare. The cost of protectionist measures is always greatest for the country imposing them.

One of the clearest indications to date of the determination of the trading nations to reverse the downward trend is the decision of GATT's Contracting Parties to convene at Ministerial Level in November this year. As you may know, ministerial meetings in the GATT have been rare occurrences: the last one was held in 1973. For this reason they are taken seriously, and are expected to produce results. This meeting is now the focus of our hopes that order can be restored. It will of course reaffirm the commitment of the Contracting Parties to the rules of GATT, but I think Governments appreciate that a merely verbal reaffirmation would not be enough. Mere words would confirm to the business world that governments have exhausted their capacity for constructive co-operative action and are reduced to collective incantation.

Fortunately, there seems to be a growing consensus that positive action is needed to restore confidence in the trading system and that the GATT, while by no means perfect, is the only viable instrument for such action. We must aim to reach a common understanding of the state of GATT law, and to secure the effective and universal application of the rules. We must decide where the existing procedures need improvement. And above all we must confront squarely the problems that have dominated this speech—those measures taken in the grey area to limit access to domestic markets or gain unfair advantage in export markets.

European Commission Communication to the Council: General Policy Orientation for the GATT Ministerial Meeting (November 1982)

General Background

The meeting of GATT Contracting Parties at Ministerial level next November is the first such occasion since 1973 (when the Tokyo Declaration that launched the MTN was adopted). The idea of this meeting arose from informal discussions in the Consultative Group of 18 in the GATT, was supported by the Ottawa Summit in July last year and endorsed by the GATT last November.

The original purpose, bearing in mind the economic recession, the stagnation of world trade and the increase in protectionist pressures, was to shore up the open world trading system by means of a strong political reaffirmation by Ministers responsible for trade in GATT countries of their allegiance to the international trade rules and their belief in a strong and effective GATT.

These objectives of strengthening the GATT and resisting protectionist pressures are still valid today. It is now generally recognised that a new major round of trade negotiations is not a practicable outcome of the November meeting—a point on which the Community has insisted throughout in all discussions with its partners. This does not, of course, prevent limited ad hoc understandings in one or other sector if that is generally acceptable. Neither does it prevent the establishment of a work programme to deal, in a forward-looking approach, with new problems to ensure that the GATT remains an effective organisation. The purpose would be to set in motion a process which will ensure progress in the coming years.

This communication aims to draw to the Council's attention the major issues which are likely to be raised next November and which will require the adoption of common Community positions. It also aims to respond to the interest of the European Parliament in a number of such issues, as expressed by the two Resolutions adopted during its May Session.

In transmitting this communication to the Council the Commission recalls the general free-trade sentiment, evident particularly at the Ottawa Summit, and which seemed to justify the Ministerial Meeting. It goes without saying that if certain trends which appear to put into question the international trading rules agreed upon in the GATT should be confirmed, thus changing inevitably the context in which the meeting takes place, the Commission would not fail to make any new proposals to the Council which might be necessary.

Besides the general themes which are likely to be raised during the Ministerial Meeting—and which are discussed in this communication—the Commission considers that the Community will have to make its position known on certain other points; these will be indicated at an appropriate time.

GATT Ministerial: General Themes

The matters for decision and discussion by GATT Ministers have been set out in a paper by Director-General Dunkel during April. This forsees a three-part structure:

Part One: This would be essentially political in character. Among the elements included in a political declaration would be a common assessment of the problem facing the international trading community, such as the recession and protectionism, and a reaffirmation of adherence to the GATT.

Part Two: This part would relate to substantive *decisions* to be submitted to Ministers. These decisions might be of two kinds: Ministers might either agree on particular solutions to problems or on principles and directives for the solution of problems within a specified time-frame.

Part Three: This part would relate to issues requiring further clarification and study. The *decisions* to be submitted to Ministers on these issues might call for further work and set a timetable for further discussion of the results and conclusions.

The political declaration would have a broad sweep. In addition to the points above, it would stress the need to maintain and further develop an open world market; it would also need to devote special attention to the problems of developing countries, in particular the least developed. It should mention certain macro-economic issues, eg the relationship between economic growth and trade, the trade impact of exchange rate fluctuations, and the increasing problem of structural adjustment. Some other politico/trade issues (the principle of reciprocity, trade harassment, embargoes) might be mentioned. Such a declaration subscribed to by some 80 Ministers across the world would have a positive effect, especially when accompanied by a series of action-oriented steps (Parts Two and Three).

The second part relates to action-oriented decisions. These may be partly on substance (agreements already reached which Ministers would endorse) and partly on procedure (directives to seek solutions in a given time-scale). Among the themes relevant to this part are developing country trade issues (politically very important), the safeguard clause, agriculture, and matters such as tariffs and non-tariff measures (essentially the MTN codes) and possibly dispute settlement.

The third part relates to issues which are relatively new in GATT or on which a few countries have a particular interest. It is not excluded that developing countries may wish to split this part so as to separate out issues such as services or trade-related investment problems which are not directly covered by existing GATT provisions. This would not alter the basic concept that the issues concerned are for further study. Other matters may include trade in high-technology products, textiles and certain economically distorting practices such as dual-pricing for oil and gas, export restrictions to favour domestic processing, etc.

A first draft of the text of the political declaration has been drafted and is under discussion in Geneva. The present paper deals essentially with the major issues in the second part of Mr. Dunkel's outline and suggests preliminary Community attitudes to these matters. Brief comments, at this stage, are added on some US proposals to be included in Part Three. Final positions, in the light of the evolution of preparatory work in Geneva, will need to be considered in more detail at a later date.

Developing Country Issues

It is clear that developing country pressures will intensify before the Ministerial Meeting for decisions, whether substantial or relating to the further work programme, to reflect the particular concerns of developing countries. In particular, the LDCs are likely to insist that the existing GATT Work Programme, especially in areas such as tariff escalation, quantitative restrictions and structural adjustment, be completed and receive priority attention, particularly in connection with the progress of preparations for global North/South negotiations.

The Community should adopt an understanding and positive attitude to such demands for special attention or differential treatment; but in proceeding to analyse the possibilities, in concrete terms, it will also be necessary to bear in mind a number of factors:

- While some specific actions should not be totally excluded over the next years, further reductions in the short term of tariff and non-tariff barriers to assist developing countries, over and above the implementation of Tokyo Round commitments, are not easy to envisage in present economic circumstances.

- Furthermore, the concept adopted in the Tokyo Round of non-reciprocal tariff negotiations (eg for tropical products) is unlikely in the future to be the general basis for negotiations with *all* developing countries. While the Community would continue to put emphasis on the need to give special help in the trade field to the lesser and least developed countries, and indeed to concentrate efforts on these beneficiaries, the guiding principle for relations with the more advanced LDCs would be rather different.

- For these countries the approach would be that they should increasingly accept new commitments and greater responsibilities within the GATT system from which at present they derive substantial benefits. For such countries the present concept that they are substantially exempted from trade commitments, and that high tariffs and other obstacles to access are in general fully justified because of a need to develop domestic industries, has in future to be challenged and accepted more selectively.

- Finally, the Community must bear in mind the special interests of the ACP countries, most of which are less advanced LDCs, and the impact on them of any efforts undertaken to meet the demands of LDCs generally.

Accordingly the Community should work to develop some of the concepts mentioned above, building upon the GATT decision of 28 November 1979 relating to developing countries, and with a view to elaborating with our partners an acceptable approach to these issues as part of the continuing GATT work programme. One approach will be for more advanced LDCs to open their markets to other LDCs and especially to the least developed. The Community should be ready to study other approaches, in the light of its own particular interests; but new developments which might modify or affect the existing autónomous nature of the Community's GSP would have to be considered with the greatest care—and only if some real compensation was available.

It will be vital if the Ministerial Meeting is to be politically a success for developing countries to feel that their special problems have been considered and taken into account. In this context the possibility of some progress on the safeguard clause will be important and it will be necessary to emphasise the major benefits for LDCs, as well as for all GATT countries, which will result from all aspects of the GATT system. It remains to be seen whether some limited, but specific benefits for developing countries are feasible, in addition to the generalised differential treatment they already receive through the GSP and the GATT codes.

The Safeguard Clauses

Efforts to negotiate a revised version of the GATT Safeguard Clause (Art. XIX) during the Tokyo Round were not successful. Although there were many matters of detail on which the parties to negotiate disagreed, the principal obstacle to agreement related to the issue of selective application of safeguard measures.

The Community (and the Nordic countries) had argued that any worthwhile revision of Art. XIX should take account of developments since 1947 and provide for the possibility, under conditions and procedures to be negotiated, that selective measures might be adopted in certain cases. This position was opposed on a point of principle by certain developing countries, especially in the Far East, with some support from eg. Japan and the US.

The insistence of these countries that any selective safeguard measures be subject to a procedure which apparently involved prior authorisation from a safeguards committee in Geneva was unaccaptable and made it impossible to conclude the negotiations.

Since 1979 the pressures from our partners have continued for a further effort to be made to develop new disciplines and procedures in this area. The Ministerial Meeting is now seen as the occasion when a new impetus could be given to discussions, perhaps even on the basis of an agreement on the outlines of a new safeguard clause with further negotiations to follow on the details within a given time-scale.

The Community has reacted to these ideas in a positive way, both because it recognises the political importance attached by many countries to the issue (a wide range of measures are being taken outside the scope of Art. XIX which is not altogether satisfactory); but also because some measure of agreement in this sector may well represent the best chance of a concrete development leading to Ministerial decisions in November.

Internal Community discussions have already begun on the orientations to be retained in this exercise. These discussions must continue, but it is already clear from a factual study recently undertaken in GATT that a wide range of measures is already being applied on a selective basis. This may facilitate a solution based upon a certain balance between conflicting interests; recognising on the one hand that selective measures would not be excluded a priori—in circumstances where this appears to be less restrictive for world trade—and accepting, on the other, a greater degree of transparency, as well as some surveillance, in relation to the "grey area measures" at present outside the strict scope of Art. XIX.

The precise criteria, conditions and procedures to be applied in connection with such a new approach would remain to be developed. There is clearly a danger that if too onerous a discipline is imposed, the objective of bringing all such measures under GATT scrutiny will not be achieved. Of major importance will be the manner in which the information on such measures is made available in GATT, the functions of any committee in examining them; and the remit to be given by Ministers for further, more detailed negotiations after the November meeting.

Agriculture

It has been clear for several months that agriculture will be a major theme for discussion and decision at the Ministerial conference. The Community's approach has been a prudent one, until the objectives of its partners are clearer: in any event, a new round of negotiations on agriculture is not to be envisaged.

Certain of the Community's partners consider that the GATT objectives in this sector have been much less effectively achieved than has been the case for manufactured products, and also that the GATT rules are less respected for agriculture than for industry.

The papers established by the GATT Secretariat (in particular C.G.18/W/59 Rev.1 and C.G.18/W/68) and the discussions of these papers in the C.G.18 have already made it possible to demonstrate that the position as regards trade in agricultural products in relation with GATT obligations is not altogether that which our partners have been alleging. It has also enabled us to point out that most important difference between GATT obligations for agriculture and for industry result from the existence of specific provisions which were written into the General Agreement from the beginning and which give a special status to agriculture.

The Commission is not convinced that the primary objective advanced by certain exporting third countries of reducing or even eliminating altogether the differences in the GATT rules between agriculture and industry—as well as the implementation of this concept, whether progressively or not—is any more realistic than it was 25 years ago when the GATT was revised. Nor does it consider that this would serve the real interests of the international community and of all Contracting Parties.

It believes that the effort undertaken in the C.G.18 to clarify the nature and scope of GATT rules for trade in agriculture should continue so as to decide, at an appropriate time and in full knowledge of the facts, whether further initiatives could be taken by the Contracting Parties to strengthen their co-operation in the agricultural sector and also to improve the conditions for agricultural trade in terms of access, competition and price stability.

The Commission considers that the Ministers should agree that the general objective of maintaining an open multilateral trading system is applicable to agriculture as to all other sectors of economic activity, but that it is necessary, in working towards this objective, to take account of all forms of direct and indirect protection and support, as well as of the political and economic realities which lie behind such policies.

Accordingly, the Ministers should encourage all efforts to secure better transparency for the measures taken by different Contracting Parties in the agricultural sector which have effects on access and on the competitive situation. Furthermore, it would be desirable to proceed to a thorough examination of the general waivers which exists in favour of certain Contracting Parties in the agricultural sector.

Finally, the Commission believes that the Ministers should be able to find a consensus and to resolve the issue, which was left undecided at the end of the Tokyo Round, of the institutional framework for multilateral co-operation in the field of trade in agricultural products. The preferred solution should be to establish an Agricultural Committee.

Tariffs and Non-tariff Measures

These are the traditional sectors of GATT work and Ministers will no doubt establish a continuing work programme on a number of issues.

As regards tariffs, it must be borne in mind that the concessions agreed on in the MTN are being applied progressively until 1 January 1987. The Community should express firm support for the principle that the Harmonised System be adopted by, at least, all major trading countries. This change will offer the prospect of a uniform and up-to-date tariff and statistical nomenclature, and a commitment from these partners, to adopt the new system would be most desirable.

The Community is in favour of all efforts to limit the scope of GATT negotiations which will be necessary as a consequence of these developments (impact on existing tariff concessions). This should be achieved by adopting the new nomenclature *without* modification or increase in existing tariff rates, whenever that is possible technically and consistently with avoiding an over-complex tariff.

The Council will no doubt need to consider other tariff issues at a later date, eg in connection with developing countries.

As regards non-tariff measures, the Community is already committed, by the terms of the agreements adopted during the Tokyo Round, to an ongoing review of the operation of the various codes and in some cases to new negotiations (civil aircraft sector, Government Procurement). The Community should express its willingness to enter into such negotiations with its partners in due course.

The Ministerial conference, which involves all GATT countries, is not an occasion for detailed discussion of the operation of the codes, which is the responsibility of the Signatories to each agreement. Nevertheless, Ministers will no doubt take note of progress in implementation, of the progressive application of new disciplines in major non-tariff areas and of the continued importance attached to further acceptance of these agreements by more GATT Members.

It is to be expected that our trading partners will put substantial emphasis on non-tariff measures which were not covered by Tokyo Round agreements, and in particular quantitative restrictions. Suggestions have already been made for a new Committee which would undertake a review of such restrictions with a view to justification or elimination over a period. The Council will need to revert to these issues after further examination by the competent Community fora.

Dispute Settlement

A number of our partners, particularly at Canadian initiative, consider that the present functioning of the GATT system for settling disputes is not satisfactory; and that the credibility of the whole set of international trade rules is prejudiced if disputes are not settled rapidly and effectively.

In the Community view the analysis that there is increasing resort to dispute settlement procedure and some strain in its functioning is correct. It is therefore possible to envisage that the Ministers should make appropriate reference to this situation and ask that the problems be reviewed.

However, the Community may well have differing views from its partners as to the causes of the present difficulties. We consider that to some extent these result from overhasty resort to GATT Procedures without sufficiently exploring the possibilities for bilateral accommodation; that the alleged shortcomings of the procedures may in fact reflect unrealistic expectations, eg a desire for the GATT system to solve difficulties in a semi-juridical way, with rulings that are binding on the parties or an expectation that the panel procedure can somehow solve problems of interpretation which were left unresolved in negotiations. The emphasis given to systematic and almost automatic use of GATT procedures (especially in US domestic legislation) is also a major source of tension.

In the light of these observations it should not be expected that a further review of the procedures would be likely to lead to a major change in the existing arrangements, although the possibility of agreement on some minor adjustments or a better understanding of the procedures (and of their inherent limitations) is not to be excluded. These issues should be further discussed in more detail in the appropriate Community fora.

Other Matters

The United States have expressed a strong interest in the area of *trade in services*, which by the 1970s accounted for some 25% of total exports by OECD countries (35% to 40% for some countries such as the USA and the UK). The Community should declare itself in favour of the proposed programme of detailed studies due to take place over the next couple of years in order to be in a position to assess whether and how GATT disciplines could be extended to this area. One potential difficulty is that a number of developing countries have shown reluctance to allow the GATT to deal with services.

A second topic advanced by the United States is in the area of *trade-related investment issues*. The objective could be to establish an inventory of investment regulations (performance requirements, local content rules) that may distort trade and to examine ways in which some international rules might be applied to these practices. The EEC would appear to have an interest in having some studies done in this area.

A third area of major interest to the United States, and to an extent Japan, is *trade in high technology products*. At this stage it is not clear whether the emphasis will be on reducing tariff and other barriers (as these countries may propose); or whether a study might examine more generally the potential conflict between the need for tariff protection (to encourage a nascent industry of major importance) and the desire for equal competitive opportunities in this sector.

Conclusion

The Council is asked to approve the broad orientations set out in this paper, especially as regards the chapters on developing countries, the safeguard clause and agriculture. The approach suggested is not intended to constitute a formal Council position at this stage, nor are specific decisions required at present. As further developments take place in Geneva, it will be clearly necessary to go beyond the present orientations and in greater detail. The Commission will present the necessary additional reports to the Council; but it seems already clear from the preparatory work that there is a reasonable prospect of achieving the objectives set for the Ministerial Meeting next November and of establishing a workmanlike programme for GATT in the next few years.

An extract from Representations to the Japanese Government by the European Community pursuant to Article XXIII, Paragraph 1 of the GATT, April 7th 1982

6. Article XXIII, paragraph 1(c)

This refers to the "existence of any other situation" that may cause the nullification or impairment of benefits. The European Community considers that the Japanese economy and policies display a number of features that constitute such a situation.

- Japanese industry is dominated by a small number of extremely large business groupings, which emerged in the post-war period with the tacit approval and support of the Japanese authorities. Though these groupings are made up of formally distinct parts, they have many links between them (cross shareholdings, informal arrangements, regular meetings or officers) and operate in all the major sectors of the economy (manufacturing in different areas, with a bank and a trading company in each grouping). Japanese industry is characterized secondly by sectoral oligopolies, in which major enterprises are vertically affiliated with small and medium firms in a more exclusive manner than in other industrialised countries.

  Reinforcing the tightly structured character of Japanese industry are the large number of industry associations which, either on their own or in co-operation with the supervisory authorities, exercise business regulatory functions. These tend to favour insiders.

  These phenomena extend into the distribution system as well as the manufacturing, service and external trade sectors. They have not been subject to the degree of active control and scrutiny considered necessary in Europe and North America in order to ensure effective open market access and genuinely free competition.

  The close inter-relationship between industry and finance (reflected in the major groupings) and the financial system itself in Japan, where large volumes of savings are channelled to industry, result in firms being able to operate on a low level of equity.

- The modernisation and restructuring of much Japanese industry was made possible by an historically high level of direct and indirect protection lasting well into the 1970s, enabling domestic suppliers to dominate large sectors of the economy. Japan's major industries, for example, steel, car production and electronics, were thus built up when there were extensive controls over imports and a high level of economic growth. These conditions contrast with those in which European industry is currently engaged in restructuring. While the degree of formal protection has been reduced in Japan, links between the administration and industry remain close and various forms of official "guidance" are influential in shaping the behaviour of firms. The industrial base of Japan has not had to meet the cost of rapid and painful adjustment arising from uncontrolled upsurges of competitive manufactured imports from her trading partners.

- A *sui generis* currency, in certain respects tightly controlled and which has been insulated from the outside world, the yen does not play a role internationally commensurate with the strength of the Japanese economy. It has been estimated that only around 4% of Western currency reserves are held by other governments in yen (compared with 12% in DM and 75% in US dollars). When the yen's international value has fallen this has been effective in favouring Japanese exports, but when the yen's international value has risen, this has not led to an increase in Japanese imports of manufactured goods on a scale comparable with what would have been expected in the case of other economies. The unbalanced trade impact of macro-economic policies is thus a matter of concern.

The result of this system, which is also reflected in the behaviour of individuals and between individuals and their firm, is that the Japanese economy displays a great resistance in practice to imports of manufactured products. This does not amount to total exclusion, but it differs in strength and degree from the problems to be found in exporting to any other industrialised country. In virtually no industrial sphere is a marked degree of import penetration to be found. To overcome these obstacles requires the solution of a network of problems ranging from the difficulty of recruiting adequate Japanese staff to securing the full backing of a distribution system which is not only complex in itself but financially integrated with the main domestic producers and/or the trading houses or large regional wholesalers, in a way which creates effective discrimination against foreign suppliers.

A central difficulty for a foreign firm is that if it merely exports its products, the structure of the Japanese economy and industry is such that the products are bound to remain luxury or marginal items, with little opportunity to expand market share. If the firm resorts to manufacture in Japan, this will entail not merely production expenses but great difficulties in securing sub-contractor links comparable to those enjoyed by competing Japanese firms, as well as the need to obtain full access to, and support from, the distribution network. The alternative of purchasing a Japanese company outright or of aquiring a controlling interest in a production or marketing organisation is not available in practice, in a way that is considered normal in other industrialised countries.

In consequence, whereas Japan has exported large and increasing quantities of manufactured products to the European Community, this has not applied in reverse. The Japanese system has a low propensity to import goods other than raw materials, for a series of structural reasons which make Japan distinct from her main industrialised partners. In short, due to a host of distinctive features which, though often invisible and elusive are nevertheless cumulatively telling in their impact on the outsider, the Japanese market is exceptionally difficult for foreign firms to penetrate. The European Community has thus not received the benefits which it considered it would receive when the tariff and other negotiations were entered into and, in view of the scale of Japanese exports to Europe and elsewhere, the result has not met the objective of the "reciprocal and mutually advantageous arrangements" refered to in the Preamble to the General Agreement.

Since it has sometimes been suggested on the Japanese side that the difficulties stem from a lack of effort or competitivity on the European part, it may be pointed out that EC firms do not encounter similar problems when exporting to other industrialsed countries. The European Community produces a wide range of competitive goods which it sells on world markets. In the case of the United States, for example, EC exports increased from $9.3 bn in 1970 to $37 bn in 1980. It is only as regards Japan that EC firms have been unable to achieve any significant degree of success in selling their goods and obtaining an adequate level of import penetration.

Nor is the European Community the only trading partner of Japan which encounters problems or which considers that Japan's resistance to imports of manufactured goods is of a special character. Besides the United States and other developed countries, there have been reports that industries in developing countries in the region also have experienced difficulties in placing their goods, even when competitively priced, on the Japanese market.

7. The European Community wishes to emphasise in conclusion that although there are specific issues for discussion, its central argument concerns the effect of Japanese trading and economic policies as a whole and the need to achieve a more balanced integration—commensurate with Japan's international responsibilities—of the Japanese economy with that of its main industrialised partners, and notably with the European Community. If this objective can be achieved the international trading system will be strengthened, a result which both Japan and the European Community wish to bring about.

US Position in the International Trading Arena
A Review by US Trade Representative William Brock, before a Trade Subcommittee of the House of Representatives October 28th 1981

I would like to lead off this series of oversight Hearings by calling the Committee's attention to three of the most critical issues presently affecting the position of the United States in the International Trading Arena. They are:

- the restoration of US competitiveness;
- the trade distortions caused by export financing practices; and
- the growing rôle of developing countries in international trade.

The restoration of US competitiveness

Our concern for the restoration of US competitiveness overseas is very strong. During no other period in our nation's history has our trade performance been more vital to the growth in our economy. Exports doubled as a percentage of GNP (Gross National Product) in the last 10 years so that today over 19% of all US goods are shipped to foreign markets. Export-related employment has grown several times faster than total employment in recent years and more than five million American workers are now dependent on the export of goods. More than ever, trade is part of our nation's lifeblood.

Even before this period of rapid trade expansion, the United States began to show signs of faltering competitive strength, largely as a result of domestic economic ills. Low rates of savings, investment and expenditures on R and D (Research and Development) and high rates of inflation affected the international competitiveness of American goods and contributed to a merchandise trade deficit of 24,000 million dollars or more every year since 1977.

Recent trends in US productivity and investment have weakened our ability to compete abroad and eroded our industrial base at home. While the United States has one of the highest levels of capital per worker and productivity in the world, our advantage in these areas is rapidly diminishing. A recent survey of 19 industrial countries indicated that the United States now ranks seventeenth in the rate of productivity growth and nineteenth in the rate of investment. Other surveys have indicated the US expenditures on research and development as a share of GNP have declined, while other developed countries are increasing their share of GNP allocated to research and development. The United States is losing its technological lead, and this is bound to have serious consequences for the international competitiveness of US products.

Therefore, this administration together with the congress has taken numerous steps to increase savings and investment while reducing inflation and the size of government. Our economic ills are now of such long duration that they have threatened to modify our economic behaviour permanently. Our program will make progress in reversing these ominous changes but will take time. What we can expect on the trade side is that, as progress is made in the revitalisation of our domestic economy, our international competitiveness will improve and our economy will adjust more easily to changing conditions in international markets.

The outlook for improved economic strength gives us all the more reason to take the lead in preserving the open international system of trade which offers US exporters the greatest opportunity to benefit from improved competitiveness. Likewise, it will provide other nations, particularly developing countries, with the best environment for achieving their aspirations for higher incomes and more efficient use of their resources.

The economic difficulties of the last few years have not been limited to the United States. Internal pressures to reduce access for imports have grown in both developed and developing countries as economic performance deteriorated. We, therefore, have taken the opportunity, on every available occasion, to encourage our trading partners to support an open international trading system. At major international economic meetings at the GATT (General Agreement on Tariffs and Trade) and OECD (Organisation for Economic Co-operation and Development) in June of this year, we strongly supported international co-operation to avoid any progressive erosion of the open, multilateral trading system and to fully and effectively implement the Tokyo Round agreements.

Furthermore, steps have been taken to begin to deal with a series of new, unresolved trade problems which pose major constraints to trade expansion in the 1980's. The consultative Group of 18, the GATT's high-level steering group agreed to recommend the convening of a full scale GATT Ministerial Meeting in November 1982 to examine the major trade issues of the 1980's. The OECD also has been charged by its members to report on the major trade issues of the 1980's. This issue's agenda being developed at the OECD Secretariat, and the work to be done at the GATT, will be important milestones in our efforts to bring such important areas as barriers to trade in services, trade-related investment practices, and LDC (Less Developed Country) trade under international review and agreement during the 1980's.

The distortions caused by export-financing practices of our competitors

If we are to realise fully the benefits of open trade, and if the trading system is to allocate resources efficiently on a global scale, trade flows must reflect natural competitive advantage and not government manipulation of the conditions of trade. It is a fact that governments still engage in a variety of trade-distorting practices, designed to undermine the judgment of the marketplace. Import restraints are erected to protect domestic markets from more competitive goods and services. Targeted industries are directly supported by governments enabling them to assume a strength they would not otherwise possess. Export subsidies likewise inhibit the normal competitive forces in the international marketplace.

One of the most difficult and damaging export subsidy problems facing the United States today is in the area of official export financing. As market interest rates have soared, the latitude for subsidisation through cheap official export credit has grown dramatically. Some governments have been increasingly tempted to compensate for non-competitive exports through heavily subsidised financing packages. This is particularly true, of course, with respect to big ticket items such as nuclear power plants and large commercial transportation systems where financial arrangements are an important competitive factor. Unfortunately, however, it is in just there products where the United States is very competitive and has traditionally dominated the world market.

We have been concerned, for example, with the extent of export credit subsidies permitted under current international agreements concerning such goods as aircraft, power plants, draglines, oil drilling machinery, etc. These and other high cost, capital intensive, high technology products have been developed over decades through investment in R and D and production technology, careful attention to customer service, and a commitment to quality. Yet, our producers of such goods now frequently lose sales to foreign competitors, not necessarily because the competition has a better product, but because they are able to draw on their national treasury for subsidised export financing. The annual cost of interest rate subsidies paid by the major OECD countries is estimated to have been at least 5,500 million dollars in 1980. France alone provided 2,300 million dollars of such subsidies, the UK 1,000 million dollars, Japan 566 million dollars, and the United States 315 million dollars. Clearly, these amounts must be reduced.

Accordingly, the administration has acted forcefully on the international front to reform the OECD arrangement on export credits. We have just concluded an agreement with 21 other OECD participants to increase the arrangement's minimum interest rate levels by 2.25%-2.50% points. This should result in a reduction of 20%-25% in export credit subsidies. In addition, we have for the first time won some limited acceptance of the principle that minimum interest rates sanctioned by the arrangement should be differentiated by currency; Japan and other low interest rate countries now are authorised to key their official export credit rates to their financial market rates, down to a floor of 9.25%; and the participants have agreed to meet again next March to review the entire arrangement with the objective of bringing its interest rates even more into line with market rates prevailing at the time.

Another noteworthy accomplishment was the recent decision by major producers of commercial jet aircraft to adhere to a common set of guidelines concerning the financing of such aircraft. Although the OECD "standstill" for aircraft financing contains no discipline on interest rates, these recent informal discussions with some of our major trading partners contemplate that dollar financing will be at a 12% interest rate.

These two achievements constitute the most significant improvements in international rules governing export finance since the arrangement was first signed in 1978. While we are pleased with the progress of the last few weeks, we are under no illusions that the job is finished. Export credit subsidies must be eliminated.

The administration's position is that finance must be a neutral element in international trade competition, and we are following a plan designed to return it to this appropriate position. Our plan consists of a multifaceted negotiating strategy aimed fundamentally at reducing export credit subsidisation. As part of this strategy we will press for continued reform of the OECD arrangement at the highest political level and we will explore how other trade options can be helpful. We will continue to target our resources to those sectors where financing is critical to securing the sale, and to consider a number of strategies designed to improve the competitiveness of our financing packages.

One proposal, among others, that I believe deserves consideration is an interest subsidy program which would afford us the flexibility to match the subsidised financing offers of foreign governments, particularly in those sectors where predatory financing practices will continue despite arrangement reform. The interest subsidy approach to financing could not only enable uo to neutralise financing as an element in international competition in the short-term, it could increase our negotiation leverage at future OECD arrangement discussions. In reviewing proposals that could increase the cost of export credits, careful consideration, of course, must be given to progress in the international negotiations and to our domestic economic and budgetary concerns in order to ensure that they are consistent with the broader economic objectives of the administration, including avoidance of increased federal intervention in capital markets.

Another point that needs to be emphasised is that government subsidisation of export financing for manufactured goods not only threatens US exports, but it can also seriously distort trade here in our own market. Let me note that the subsidies agreement clearly states that such assistance should not adversely affect the trade interests of others. Our companies and our trading partners should know that we are prepared to act firmly, using such available remedies as are appropriate to the particular circumstances, to ensure that goods are fairly traded in the US market without being dumped or subsidised in an injurious way.

Essential to our efforts on both the international and domestic fronts is working closely with the congress so that a lasting solution to the trade distorting practice of subsidised export credits can be reached quickly and US exporters will no longer be unfairly penalised.

US trade relations with developing countries

Free international competition in an open, global trading system is in the economic interest of all countries, not only the United States. The free flow of goods and services provides an ever-increasing market for all trading nations. Subsidisation, either of exports or export financing, prevents resources from being efficiently allocated and narrows the range of economic opportunities for citizens in all countries. That said, we would be naive to think that some countries are not delighted to buy exports subsidised by the taxpayers in another country. This is especially true in the case of credit subsidisation for exports to developing countries, for whom high borrowing costs are a serious drag on development plans. This is short sighted, however, as scarce international resources will end up in second or third-best uses and tomorrow everyone, including developing countries, will be paying unnecessarily high prices for today's subsidised goods.

Following last week's summit in Cancun much attention is being focused on developing countries' economies. I would like to elaborate on the contribution trade makes to foreign economic development and what rôle the United States has played in spurring this process.

Developing countries experienced an impressive expansion in trade during the last decade. The volume of exports from the oil importing developing countries grew at an average annual rate of 6.3% in the 1970's compared to average annual growth of 5.5% for industrial countries. However, trade expansion in the Third World, especially in the manufacturing sector, has been highly concentrated among less than a dozen countries.

The sharp differences among LDC's trade performance despite comparable access to international markets suggests that the policies and circumstances of the individual LDCs are the major determinants of trade success. This hypothesis was confirmed during a 10-nation trip I took to Asia this summer. In the space of a month I met with the finance, trade and agriculture ministers of these countries and in many cases with their heads of state. I was particularly struck by the dynamic growth of the ASEAN (Association of Southwest Asian Nations), nations which today constitute our fifth largest trading partner. Total trade between the United States and the ASEAN countries has nearly tripled since 1974. Should these unusually high rates of growth continue, the ASEAN countries could be our number one trading partner by the end of this century.

I found a number of trade policies common to many of these ASEAN countries which merit review. Foremost among these policies was the progressive elimination of economic rigidities induced by import substitution and export subsidisation policies, greater domestic reliance on the free market, encouragement of foreign direct investment through forums such as the US-ASEAN Business Council and, with the exception of Thailand, which is considering accession, through active participation in the GATT. Again, the critical ingredient to success appears to be a willingness to maintain open markets. The United States will continue to encourage the progressive reduction of trade barriers in our major LDC trading partners, and especially in the more advanced economies.

The US contribution to LDC trade expansion over the past decade should be viewed in terms of a consistent commitment to open markets—a position sometimes not shared by some of our major industrial trading partners. Historically, the United States has provided one of the most open markets in the world. The average duty collected on dutiable imports has been 10% or lower since 1970. In 1980 the average duty collected was 5.5%. When we complete the implementation of our MTN (Multilateral Trade Negotiations) Tariff reductions, this rate will fall to approximately 4% for industrial products. US quantitative restrictions on imports are few, and our customs procedures are highly transparent and predictable.

In addition to the general openness of our market, for the past six years the United States has maintained the generalised system of preferences (GSP), which provides developing countries with preferential duty-free treatment on many products. Although the overall volume of trade affected by the US GSP is quite small, it is generally felt that the program has helped developing countries diversify their economies and increase export earnings. This development through trade lessens developing country need for external aid and promotes the fuller integration of developing countries in the international trading system.

Statutory authority for the US GSP expires in January 1985. The administration has decided to seek an extension of that authority, but before submitting extension legislation to congress we will take a fresh look at the program's purpose, its rôle within overall US trade policy with the developing countries, its operation, and its impact on different beneficiaries. In this connection, the administration will work closely with the Congress. In addition, we plan to conduct public hearings next Spring throughout the United States in which we will solicit comments from all interested parties on the GSP. We would hope to be able then to put together a program closely tailored to LDC needs and US trade goals in the 1980's.

The administration will take advantage of this introspective period to explore with the other 18 GSP donor countries the feasibility of developing an internationally harmonised GSP program. At present the operational aspects of the major programs differ widely, placing an unnecessary burden on LDC exporters. We will take the initiative—and in fact have already begun informal consultations with the EC (European Community) and Japan—in seeking a simplification of the international GSP network.

The foreign exchange that developing countries earn through trade dwarfs the funds available to them through development assistance. In 1980, for example, the value of exports from the non-OPEC (Non-Oil Exporting) developing countries to the United States (63,400 million dollars) was more than twice as great as total net official development assistance received by developing countries from all bilateral and multilateral sources combined. In the past two years alone, the non-OPEC developing countries have earned more from exports to the United States (114,500 million dollars) than the entire Third World has received from the World Bank in the 36 years of that Institution's existence.

Trade's contribution to development can be enhanced substantially by complementary flows of private investment and development assistance. Such an integrated and complementary development perspective plays a vital role in the Caribbean basin initiative. As you know, I have been charged with designing and co-ordinating a pilot development plan tailored to the specific needs of the Caribbean.

During the past few months the administration has engaged in intensive analysis and developed numerous options in consultation with other concerned countries, interested private groups and potential beneficiaries. I am excited about three aspects of our approach. First, we are trying to combine trade, aid, and investment tools to provide an effective stimulant for growth. Secondly, we realise that to be successful we must limit the rôle of our government and engage the vitality and energy of the private sector. Thirdly, this is the first endeavour of which I am aware, where we are working with other donor countries, including some at different levels of economic development, to assist a particular region. We are ready to make a major effort, and I will soon be bringing specific proposals to the congress for consideration by this sub-committee.

My comments thus far have focused on what contribution trade has made to development in the Third World. This process has been encouraged every step of the way by the United States. We have done so not only because this country traditionally has taken a great interest in helping those in need to reach their development goals. We have also done so because economic growth abroad translates into economic strength at home. Developing countries provide the fastest growing markets for US exports. For the period 1973-1980 real GNP grew at an average annual rate of 5% in oil-importing developing countries compared to an average annual growth rate of just 2% in industrial countries. The products that these dynamic economies are absorbing—capital goods and heavy machinery as well as agricultural products—are just those items in which the United States is extremely competitive in the international market. During the 1970's oil-importing developing countries absorbed about one-quarter of all US exports of manufactures and this share is increasing. At the same time, these countries buy approximately one-third of all our agricultural shipments. It's very simple. The more we encourage their development, the more they will encourage ours.

One other point should be raised concerning the importance of developing country economies to the economic health of the United States. The oil shocks of the past several years have very severely affected the foreign payments accounts of oil-importing LDCs. The aggregate annual current account deficit for these countries rose from 37,000 million dollars in 1978 to 82,000 million dollars in 1980 and may reach 97,000 million dollars this year. Outstanding medium and long-term debt of LDC's has risen substantially and surpassed 425,000 million dollars in 1980, of which oil-importing LDCs accounted for 300,000 million dollars. A great deal of this debt is held by US banks.

The openness of industrial markets to LDC exports is not just essential to LDC prospects for growth but also to their ability to meet their international financial obligations and to finance future borrowings. If substantial financial resources are going to continue to flow to LDC borrowers, then trade policy should help keep risks in an acceptable range by maintaining open markets for LDC exports. LDCs require substantial export earnings to meet debt obligations. Furthermore, private creditors in the future will be unlikely to expand their lending to countries with poor export performances. The administration's trade policy which promotes open markets both in the United States and abroad must be characterised as one of the soundest guarantees for outstanding LDC loans and for the smooth operation of the international financial system in the future.

It most certainly is in the economic interest of the United States to encourage further developing country participation in the international trading system. We cannot afford to have those markets which are so important to the vitality of the US economy operating outside the accepted rules of international trade. In this regard, the United States took the lead during the MTN in encouraging developing country participation in bilateral tariff agreements as well as in the multilateral non-tariff measures codes. Our efforts will continue. The 1982 GATT ministerial provides an excellent opportunity to strengthen this process. We intend to work closely with developing countries in preparing for the ministerial and we hope that the post-ministerial work plan will lay the groundwork for more active, responsible participation by developing countries in the GATT during the next decade.

US trade policy faces great challenges in the next couple of years. But I consider these challenges as opportunities to broaden and increase the export potential of the US economy. The administration cannot do this alone, however. I intend to work closely with each of you in the months ahead in order to ensure that this goal is met.

Priority Trade Issues for the '80's

A Statement before the House Ways and Means Committee
October 29th 1981

At yesterday's (October 28) session, I discussed the issues of US competitiveness, export credits, and the rôle of developing countries in international trade. These areas will continue to be important during the 1980's. In particular, the developing nations will play an important part in the world trading system and must be considered as we formulate our trade objectives. Today, I would like to discuss a series of additional issues that will demand our attention during this decade.

GATT Ministerial Meeting

Before I begin to discuss specific issues, I would like to stress this administration's strong support for the meeting of GATT at the ministerial level that is being planned for November 1982. This will present an excellent opportunity for the trading nations to reach consensus on the major trade issues of the 80's and to initiate solutions to the problems we face. It will be important for the ministers to review the effectiveness of the various codes negotiated during the Tokyo Round of Multilateral Trade Negotiations (MTN), with a view to identifying areas where adjustments may be warranted. In addition, we must find ways to begin resolving trade problems that we have not dealt with, or inadequately dealt with, in previous negotiations.

Planning for the ministerial will continue at the meeting of the GATT council on November 3 and the matter will be brought to the meeting of the contraction parties (CP's) in Geneva during the week of November 23. We anticipate that the CP's will unanimously endorse the ministerial, just as the GATT consultative group of 18 did at their meeting two weeks ago. We welcome the views of the congress as we prepare for the ministerial meeting in the coming months.

In conjunction with ministerial planning, the MTN codes on technical barriers to trade (standards) and government procurement will be coming up for renegotiation in 1983 and 1984, respectively. During this time period, we will also be examining the possibility of negotiation of a new worldwide tariff nomenclature, the harmonised system. By the time of the ministerial, I would also hope that we could see the results of ongoing negotiations on commercial counterfeiting and safeguards.

Tariffs

As you know, the administration is seeking a two-year extension of the President's tariff negotiating authority (under Section 124 of the Trade Act of 1974) which expires on January 3, 1982. We believe that it is vital for the President to retain such authority so that he may be able to take advantage of negotiating opportunities as they develop and to pursue improved market access for US goods abroad. We also believe that the current limitations and procedural requirements of the Section 124 authority are sufficient safeguards for those industries concerned about injurious import competition. The recently concluded US-Japanese semiconductor negotiations, which will bring Japanese tariffs in conformity with US tariffs, are an outstanding example of an improvement in foreign market access resulting from our use of Section 124. During the next two years the administration also plans to conduct a general review of its longer-term needs for such tariff authority.

As I mentioned earlier, another major trade issue during the 1980's and one which could have far-reaching implications for US and foreign tariffs, is the harmonised system for the classification of goods in international trade. This new nomenclature system is scheduled to be considered for adoption by countries beginning in 1983 but would not be put into effect before 1985. During the next few years, the United States will need to thoroughly analyse the impact of the harmonised system. The President recently asked the US International Trade Commission to prepare a draft conversion of our tariff schedules into the format of the harmonised system so that we can assess the effects of adoption on US tariffs and on US industries, workers and trade.

Services

The United States must continue its active leadership in seeking to liberalise trade in services. Services trade accounts for a substantial portion of US exports and represents an area of rapid economic growth. Continued growth, however, will depend upon our service industries having greater access to foreign markets. Presently there exists a wide variety of trade barriers to services which limit world trade in services and the benefits which accrue from it. In the past there has not been a systematic means of addressing services trade issues, resolving services trade problems, or reducing services trade barriers. Unlike trade in goods, nations have not established a body of international agreements concerning fair trade in services.

There is a great need to build an international framework for resolving trade problems in services which would establish internationally agreed-upon rules and procedures for services, and provide for both bilateral and multilateral approaches to issues. We have been working to lay the necessary groundwork for the development of such a framework and I intend to vigorously pursue this objective. It is a process of familiarising trade partners with our mutual interests in this area while building a consensus among interested nations as to the best means of approaching the problem.

Some have argued that there are too many problems to resolve in manufacturers and agricultural trade to undertake a complicated and time-consuming exercise in services. I disagree. Countries are rapidly becoming more service-dominated, and there is simply too much at stake for us to delay the inevitable process of insuring that world markets are open and the rules of trade are clarified in this area.

Agriculture

One of our most important goals of the 80's is to remove obstacles to trade in agriculturul products. As the world's most efficient producer of a whole host of farm products, we have a great stake in assuring a free and open trading system for these goods. We recognise, however, that agricultural policy is often an extension of social policy and the actions that many governments take in the farm sector are not necessarily the product of economic logic. This makes our task infinitely more difficult, but it doesn't reduce our resolve that distortions in agricultural trade must be eliminated.

Our exports—and those of other countries—are facing the double threat of import barriers—both tariff and non-tariff—raised by a number of countries, as well as displacement and reduced export potentials stemming from the subsidised exports of other major trading nations. It is difficult to say which is the most detrimental to our trade, but the export subsidies offend my sense of fair play.

We have found in too many instances that our private sector has developed a market for a particular product in a particular country, only to lose that market to subsidised shipments from a third country. I am truly irritated when I see our private sector competing against the treasuries of other nations. It's just not right, and we intend to press our case in the GATT.

My office has before it now several complaints against the European Community's export subsidy practices. We have already begun the dispute settlement process on two complaints—wheat flour and sugar—within the subsidies code that was negotiated during the multilateral trade negotiations. Others will be processed over the next few months. We will be writing new GATT case law, as ours will be the first complaints brought under the code. Since we will be breaking new ground, we will be setting the stage for other cases to follow. This will be an important factor in our own approach and the approach that others will follow with respect to the subsidies code, their own export practices, and the GATT.

It is the attitude with respect to the GATT that we feel is very important. There are some who say that the GATT simply doesn't work for agriculture and who will cite export subsidies as an area in which farm products are treated differently. We, of course, feel that agriculture is as much a part of the GATT as are industrial goods or services, and we will continue to press for agriculture's inclusion in all aspects of the GATT. We recognise that for reasons of social policy, governments will continue to undertake special programs in the agricultural area; therefore, we need a way to convince all governments that a more open and economically rational agricultural system is in their own self interest. I repeat . . . in their own self interest. I am emphasising this because I frankly think that no amount of debate will convince a nation to change any policy, particularly one so emotionally charged as agriculture, unless it perceives some benefit for its citizens in doing so.

That is the challenge—how do we get the issue addressed, and how do we devise systems that protect the socio-economic interests of governments and at the same time open markets and reduce subsidised exports? I don't have the answer to the second part of the challenge, but I think the GATT ministerial will be an appropriate and excellent forum for the first. Having agriculture discussed by the trade ministers would be only the first step. I think the GATT would have to agree to undertake a work program that would have as its ultimate goal, the substantial reduction of distortions to trade in agricultural products.

There are a few specific areas where we will work to remove barriers in the early years of this decade. One such area of concentration will be agricultural trade with Japan. Two long-standing problems that we intend to resolve are Japanese limitations on the importation of citrus and beef. Both were the subject of some liberalisation in the MTN and are scheduled for future discussions. We will press for the removal of these barriers.

Other market access issues will be given high priority as well, but we will also work to maintain the access that we have already negotiated and paid for. Our position has been made clear and I don't wish to engage in rhetoric on the matter of our market in the European Community for soya beans and non-grain feed ingredients. Suffice it to say that we value the concessions that we received in earlier trade negotiations. We do not wish to bear the EC's burden for structural adjustment. It is the EC's price support system that makes its domestic grain prices so high that the lower-priced imported alternatives are attractive.

This administration has proposed substantial changes in our own domestic agricultural programs. The Congress has adopted an overall program that is different from that which existed 20 years ago. More remains to be done, but we're taking Uncle Sam out of farming and returning it to the people who know how to do it best—the farmers. This will cause some upheaval and there are likely to be some negative political consequences, but we and the Congress had to make some courageous moves in order to put our economic house in order. The changes that will come about as a result of these structural adjustments will be virtually universally positive. The result should be an agricultural machine driven by market forces. The American farmer, unfettered by restraints on his productive capabilities, will be in a position to take advantage of his productivity to produce increased quantities of goods for the domestic and international market. Our economic program should go a long way towards making this possible—but the other key element in making this work is to assure the producer that he will have access to markets for that production. I pledge myself to make every effort to assure that those markets will be there.

Investment

Investment policy is an important area of growing concern to us in the maintenance of an open world trading system. Government intervention in the investment area increasingly threatens to negate the trade liberalisation which has been accomplished over the past 30 years. Foreign governments impose disincentives and barriers to investment and discriminate against foreign investors. These investment problems, which exist both with LCD's and some industrial countries, reflect an economic protectionism and nationalism that is detrimental to the future vitality of the world economy.

Many developed and developing countries impose performance requirements as a condition for approval of new investment or receipt of investment incentives. Examples include import substitution, local content, and export performance requirements which distort or block trade as effectively as tariffs or non-tariff trade barriers. These trade-related performance requirements are a new form of non-tariff barriers which the GATT should address. We have begun preparatory work on performance requirements in the OECD, the GATT, and the OME/IBRD and we hope to have countries address this issue seriously as part of any future work program. Our objective is to obtain a consensus on rules to restrict the imposition of performance requirements.

Addressing the need for additional foreign investment in developing countries is also a particularly high priority issue for the administration. We believe that a more free capital flow can greatly improve the development prospects of third world countries. We are attempting to co-ordinate a program of increased investment in the Carribbean and other developing areas through strengthened OPIC activities, a suggested multilateral approach to international investment insurance, and bilateral investment treaties. An approach which strengthens the private sector, both domestic and foreign, in the LDC's will help stabilise their economies and governments and rebound to the economic and political benefit of the United States.

This administration intends to pursue a vigorous and positive investment policy, emphasising the liberalisation of investment barriers to US investment abroad while maintaining our open investment climate domestically, and in particular focussing on the positive development aspects of easier flows of investment to developing countries. An open investment environment is an essential complement to an open trading system.

High technology goods

One of the major trade issues in the 1980's will be trade in high technology goods, including computers, telecommunications, nuclear energy, robotics, fiber optics, pharmaceuticals, and biotechnology.

Our key trade competitors recognise the importance of high technology industries to their plans for economic growth and national security. Unfortunately, many have sought to foster development of such industries by interfering with the operation of normal market forces to ensure special treatment of high technology industries. Preferential tax policies, intervention in capital markets, as well as trade and investment policies have all been used to accommodate these efforts.

In the EC for example, the tariff on semiconductors is 17% as opposed to the 4.2% as was recently negotiated by the United States and Japan. The EC rules of origin add an equivalent of an additional 3%-5% duty for US-made components. The EC telecommunication agencies are partially or wholly government owned or cotrolled and were excluded from coverage in the government procurement code, resulting in very limited market access for US exporters. These protective measures are coupled with export promotion programs, such as subsidised export financing.

In Japan there is a high degree of industry co-operation in research and development, which is helped by government priority setting, which directs capital to high-risk areas. Japanese government assistance to the computer industry has included development of industry consortiums, government-funded development of a high-performance computer, and tax benefits for computer users to encourage purchases. All these actions have very profound trade effects.

There is a growing concern that US high technology industries will face an unfair competitive disadvantage as a result of these policies and they may suffer substantial loss of international markets over the next few years. The US high technology industries are competitive and contribute disproportionately to US export performance, growth, and productivity in the domestic economy. These industries provide support to our national defence and hold the key to America's competitiveness in the 1980's and 1990's. We cannot afford to lose our lead in this area.

As opposed to taking a primarily reactive approach to sectoral problems, the US government would like to adopt a more forward-looking approach in the high technology industries—a preventative perspective both domestically and internationally. Our objective will be a mutual reduction of trade distortions to ensure a more free and open trading system. The current three-way competition between Japan, the United States and the EC in semiconductors foreshadows increasingly fierce competition in the high technology arena in the next decade.

The high technology industries will be a major concern of US trade policy in the decade ahead. These are industries that we are competitive in, in terms of technology, price and quality. US industries are not intimidated by competition, as long as it is fair and they feel secure that they can maintain their lead in a free trade environment. The US government is committed to ensuring that a free trade environment exists and to taking an aggressive posture where needed to further that end.

Conclusion

I have addressed the priority trade issues that the United States will face in the decade of the 80's. This is not an exhaustive inventory, as we must contend with a myriad of problems on an ongoing basis. Furthermore, we must continue to maintain open markets at home as we seek to expand market access for US goods and services abroad. The United States must respond to trade issues promptly and vigorously within a cohesive overall national trade policy framework, based on a commitment to continued liberalisation of global trade.

Members of the British-North American Committee

Chairmen
SIR ALASTAIR DOWN
Chairman,
Burmah Oil Company,
Swindon, Wiltshire

WILLIAM L. WEARLY
Chairman, Executive Committee,
Ingersoll-Rand Company,
Woodcliff Lake, New Jersey

Chairman, Executive Committee
WILLIAM I. M. TURNER, JR.
President and Chief Executive Officer,
Consolidated-Bathurst Inc.,
Montreal, Quebec

Members
R. W. ADAM
Deputy Chairman,
The British Petroleum Company Limited,
London

WLLIAM M. AGEE
Chairman and Chief Executive Officer,
The Bendix Corporation,
Southfield, Michigan

J. A. ARMSTRONG
Toronto, Ontario

DAVID ATTERTON
Chairman,
Foseco Minsep Ltd.,
London

CHARLES F. BAIRD
Chairman and Chief Executive Officer,
INCO Limited,
Toronto, Ontario

JOSEPH E. BAIRD
Los Angeles, California

R. J. BALL
Chairman,
Legal & General Assurance Group Ltd.,
and Principal,
London Business School,
London

ROBERT A. BANDEEN
Chairman and President,
Crown Life Insurance Company,
Toronto, Ontario

SIR DONALD BARRON
Chairman,
Midland Bank Limited, London

CARL E. BEIGIE
President,
C. D. Howe Institute,
Toronto, Ontario

MICHEL BELANGER
Chairman of the Board,
President and Chief Executive Officer,
National Bank of Canada,
Montreal, Quebec

C. FRED BERGSTEN
Director,
Institute for International Economics,
Washington, D.C.

CARROL D. BOLEN
President,
Illinois-Wisconsin Division,
Pioneer Hi-Bred International, Inc.,
Princeton, Illinois

JOHN F. BOOKOUT
President and Chief Executive Officer,
Shell Oil Company, Houston, Texas

FRANK BORMAN
Chairman, President and Chief Executive
Officer,
Eastern Airlines, Miami, Florida

THORNTON F. BRADSHAW
Chairman of the Board and Chief
Executive Officer,
RCA Corporation, New York, N.Y.

F. S. BURBIDGE
Chairman and Chief Executive Officer,
Canadian-Pacific Limited,
Montreal, Quebec

JAMES W. BURNS
President,
Power Corporation of Canada Ltd.,
Montreal, Quebec

SIR RICHARD BUTLER
President,
National Farmers' Union, London

VISCOUNT CALDECOTE
Chairman,
Delta Metal Company, and
Chairman,
Finance for Industry, London

SILAS S. CATHCART
Chairman,
Illinois Tool Works, Inc.,
Chicago, Illinois

HAROLD VAN B. CLEVELAND
Vice President,
Citibank, N.A., New York, N.Y.

DONALD M. COX
Director and Senior Vice President,
Exxon Corporation, New York, N.Y.

FRANK J. CUMMISKEY
Greenwich, Connecticut

JAMES W. DAVANT
Chairman of the Board,
Paine Webber Incorporated,
New York, N.Y.

RALPH P. DAVIDSON
Chairman,
Time Incorporated,
New York, N.Y.

A. H. A. DIBBS
Deputy Chairman,
National Westminster Bank Limited,
London

SIR RICHARD DOBSON
Richmond, Surrey

WILLIAM DODGE
Ottawa, Ontario

WILLIAM H. DONALDSON
Chairman and Chief Executive,
Donaldson Enterprises Inc.,
New York, N.Y.

PETER P. DONIS
Executive Vice President,
Caterpillar Tractor Company,
Peoria, Illinois

EDWARD DONLEY
Chairman,
Air Products and Chemicals Inc.,
Allentown, Pennsylvania

ALLAN R. DRAGONE
President and Chief Operating Officer,
Celanese Corporation, New York, N.Y.

GEOFFREY DRAIN
General Secretary,
National Association of Local
Government Officers, London

JOHN DU CANE
Director,
AMAX Inc., London

TERRY DUFFY
President,
Amalgamated Union of Engineering
Workers, London

KEN DURHAM
Chairman,
Unilever Ltd., London

GERRY EASTWOOD
General Secretary,
Association of Patternmakers and
Allied Craftsmen, London

HARRY E. EKBLOM
Chairman and Chief Executive Officer,
European American Bancorp,
New York, N.Y.

MOSS EVANS
General Secretary,
Transport and General Workers' Union,
London

JOCK K. FINLAYSON
President,
The Royal Bank of Canada,
Toronto, Ontario

GLENN FLATEN
President,
Canadian Federation of Agriculture,
Regina, Saskatchewan

C. S. FLENNIKEN
President and Chief Executive Officer,
Canadian International Paper Company,
Montreal, Quebec

RICHARD W. FOXEN
Corporate Vice President—International,
Rockwell International Corp.,
Pittsburgh, Pennsylvania

SIR ALISTAIR FRAME
Deputy Chairman and Chief Executive,
Rio-Tinto Zinc Corporation, London

THEODORE GEIGER
Distinguished Research Professor of
Intersocietal Relations,
School of Foreign Service, Georgetown
University, Washington, D.C.

GWAIN GILLESPIE
Senior Vice President—Finance and
Administration,
Heublein Inc., Farmington, Connecticut

MALCOLM GLENN
Executive Vice President,
Reed Holdings Incorporated,
Rickmansworth, Herts.

GEORGE GOYDER
Sudbury, Suffolk

JOHN H. HALE
Senior Vice President,
Alcan Aluminium Limited,
Montreal, Quebec

HON. HENRY HANKEY
British Secretary,
BNAC, Westerham, Kent

AUGUSTIN S. HART, JR.
Director,
Quaker Oats Company, Chicago, Illinois

FRED L. HARTLEY
Chairman and President,
Union Oil Company of California,
Los Angeles, California

PAUL HAZEN
Vice Chairman,
Wells Fargo and Company,
Marina del Ray, California

G. R. HEFFERNAN
President,
Co-Steel International Ltd.,
Whitby, Ontario

ROBERT HENDERSON
Chairman,
Kleinwort Benson Ltd., London

SIR TREVOR HOLDSWORTH
Chairman
Guest, Keen & Nettlefolds Ltd., London

HENDRIK S. HOUTHAKKER
Professor of Economics,
Harvard University, Cambridge,
Massachusetts

DONALD P. JACOBS
Dean,
J. L. Kellogg Graduate School of
Management, Northwestern University,
Evanston, Illinois

JOHN V. JAMES
Chairman of the Board and
Chief Executive Officer,
Dresser Industries, Inc., Dallas, Texas

GEORGE S. JOHNSTON
President,
Scudder, Stevens & Clark, New York, N.Y.

JOSEPH D. KEENAN
President,
Union Label and Service Trades
Department, AFL-CIO, Washington, D.C.

C. CALVERT KNUDSEN
Chairman and Chief Executive Officer,
MacMillan, Bloedel Limited
Vancouver, B.C.

H. U. A. LAMBERT
Chairman,
Barclays Bank International Ltd., London

INGRAM LENION
Managing Director,
The Bowater Corporation Ltd., London

WILLIAM A. LIFFERS
Vice Chairman,
American Cyanamid Company,
Wayne, New Jersey

FRANKLIN A. LINDSAY
Chairman, Executive Committee,
Itek Corporation, Lexington,
Massachusetts

SIR PETER MACADAM
Chairman,
B.A.T. Industries Ltd., London

IAN MacGREGOR
Honorary Chairman,
AMAX Inc., Greenwich, Connecticut

CARGILL MacMILLAN, JR.
Senior Vice President,
Cargill Inc., Minneapolis, Minnesota

J. P. MANN
Deputy Chairman,
United Biscuits (Holdings) Ltd.,
Isleworth, Middlesex

WILLIAM A. MARQUARD
Chairman, President and Chief Executive
Officer,
American Standard Inc., New York, N.Y.

A. B. MARSHALL
Chairman
Bestobell Ltd., London

WILLIAM J. McDONOUGH
Chairman, Asset and Liability
Management Committee,
The First National Bank of Chicago,
Chicago, Illinois

DONALD K. McIVOR
Chairman and Chief Executive Officer,
Imperial Oil Limited, Toronto, Ontario

DONALD E. MEADS
Chairman and President,
Carver Associates,
Plymouth Meeting, Pennsylvania

SIR PATRICK MEANEY
Group Managing Director,
Thomas Tilling Limited, London

SIR PETER MENZIES
Welwyn, Hertfordshire

JOHN MILLER
Vice Chairman,
National Planning Association,
Washington, D.C.

ALLEN E. MURRAY
President of Marketing and Refining
Division,
Mobil Oil Corporation, New York, N.Y.

KENNETH D. NADEN
President,
National Council of Farmer Cooperatives.
Washington, D.C.

J. W. NEWALL
Chairman, President and
Chief Executive Officer,
Du Pont Canada Inc.,
Mississauga, Ontario

DR. CONOR CRUISE O'BRIEN
Dublin, Ireland

WILLIAM S. OGDEN
Vice Chairman and
Chief Financial Officer,
The Chase Manhattan Bank, N.A.,
New York, N.Y.

ANTHONY J. F. O'REILLY
President and Chief Executive Officer,
H.J. Heinz Company,
Pittsburgh, Pennsylvania

PAUL L. PARKER
Executive Vice President,
General Mills, Inc.,
Minneapolis, Minnesota

BROUGHTON PIPKIN
Stow-on-the-Wold, Gloucestershire

GEORGE J. POULIN
General Vice President,
International Association of Machinists &
Aerospace Workers, Washington, D.C.

SIR RICHARD POWELL
Hill Samuel Group Ltd., London

ALFRED POWIS
Chairman,
Noranda Mines Limited, Toronto, Ontario

PAUL E. PRICE
Executive Vice President,
Direct-to-Consumer,
Businesses and Chemicals,
Quaker Oats Company, Chicago, Illinois

LOUIS PUTZE
Ligonier, Pennsylvania

MERLE R. RAWSON
Chairman and Chief Executive Officer,
The Hoover Company,
North Canton, Ohio

GRANT L. REUBER
Deputy Chairman,
Bank of Montreal, Montreal, Quebec

BEN ROBERTS
Professor of Industrial Relations,
London School of Economics, London

HAROLD B. ROSE
Group Economic Advisor,
Barclays Bank Limited, London

CHESTER A. SADLOW
President,
Europe/Africa/Middle East,
Westinghouse Electric Corporation,
Pittsburgh, Pennsylvania

DAVID SAINSBURY
Director of Finance,
J. Sainsbury Ltd., London

WILLIAM R. SALOMON
Limited Partner and Honorary Member
of the Executive Committee,
Salomon Brothers, New York, N.Y.

A. C. I. SAMUEL
Handcross, Sussex

HOWARD SAMUEL
President,
Industrial Union Department AFL-CIO,
Washington, D.C.

NATHANIEL SAMUELS
Chairman, Advisory Director,
Lehman Brothers Kuhn Loeb Inc.

LORD SEEBOHM
Dedham, Essex

THE EARL OF SELKIRK
President,
Royal Central Asian Society, London

JACOB SHEINKMAN
Secretary-Treasurer,
Amalgamated Clothing & Textile
Workers' Union, New York, N.Y.

LORD SHERFIELD
Director,
Badger Limited, Brentford, Middlesex

R. MICHAEL SHIELDS
Managing Director,
Associated Newspapers Group Ltd.,
London

GEORGE L. SHINN
Chairman and Chief Executive Officer,
The First Boston Corporation,
New York, N.Y.

GORDON R. SIMPSON
Chairman,
General Accident Fire and
Life Assurance Corporation Ltd.,
Perth, Scotland

SIR ROY SISSON
Chairman,
Smiths Industries Limited, London

SIR LESLIE SMITH
Chairman,
BOC International Ltd., London

E. NORMAN STAUB
Director, Retired Chairman,
The Northern Trust Company,
Chicago, Illinois

RALPH I. STRAUS
New York, N.Y.

SIR ROBERT TAYLOR
Deputy Chairman,
Standard Chartered Bank Ltd., London

JAMES C. THACKRAY
President,
Bell Canada,
Montreal, Quebec

WILLIAM C. THOMSON
A Managing Director,
Royal Dutch/Shell Group of Companies,
London

ALEXANDER C. TOMLINSON
President,
National Planning Association,
Washington, D.C.

ALAN TUFFIN
General Secretary,
Union of Communication Workers,
London

J. C. TURNER
General President,
International Union of Operating
Engineers, AFL-CIO, Washington, D.C.

W. O. TWAITS
Toronto, Ontario

MARTHA REDFIELD WALLACE
Director,
The Henry Luce Foundation Inc.,
New York, N.Y.

GLENN E. WATTS
President,
Communication Workers of America,
AFL-CIO, Washington, D.C.

VISCOUNT WEIR
Vice Chairman,
The Weir Group Limited,
Cathcart, Scotland

FREDERICK B. WHITTEMORE
Managing Director,
Morgan Stanley & Co. Incorporated,
New York, N.Y.

CHARLES WOOTTON
Senior Director, Foreign and Domestic,
Policy Analysis and Planning,
Gulf Oil Corporation
Pittsburgh, Pennsylvania

Sponsoring Organisations

The British-North American Research Association was inaugurated in December 1969. Its primary purpose is to sponsor research on British-North American economic relations in association with the British-North American Committee. Publications of the British-North American Research Association as well as publications of the British-North American Committee are available from the Association's office, 1 Gough Square, London EC4A 3DE (Tel. 01-353 6371). The Association is recognised as a charity and is governed by a Council under the chairmanship of Sir Alastair Down.

National Planning Association is an independent, private, nonprofit, non-political organization that carries on research and policy formulation in the public interest. NPA was founded during the Great Depression of the 1930s when conflicts among the major economic groups—business, labour, agriculture—threatened to paralyze national decision-making on the critical issues confronting American society. It was dedicated to the task of getting these diverse groups to work together to narrow areas of controversy and broaden areas of agreement and to provide on specific problems, concrete programs for action planned in the best traditions of a functioning democracy. Such democratic planning, NPA believes, involves the development of effective governmental and private policies and programs not only by official agencies, but also through the independent initiative and co-operation of the main private-sector groups concerned. And, to preserve and strengthen American political and economic democracy, the necessary government actions have to be consistent with, and stimulate the support of, a dynamic private sector.

NPA brings together influential and knowledgeable leaders from business, labour, agriculture, and the applied and academic professions to serve on policy committees. These committees identify emerging problems confronting the nation at home and abroad and seek to develop and agree upon policies and programs for coping with them. The research and writing for these committees are provided by NPA's professional staff and, as required, by outside experts.

In addition, NPA's professional staff undertakes research designed to provide data and ideas for policy makers and planners in government and the private sector. These activities include the preparation on a regular basis of economic and demographic projections for the national economy, regions, states, metropolitan areas, and counties; research on national goals and priorities, productivity and economic growth, welfare and dependency problems, employment and manpower needs, energy and environmental questions, and other economic and social problems confronting American society; and analyses and forecasts of changing international realities and their implications for US policies.

NPA publications, including those of the British-North American Committee, can be obtained from the Association's office, 1606 New Hampshire Avenue, N.W., Washington, D.C. 20009 (Tel. 202-265-7685). **The C.D. Howe Institute** was established in 1973 by the merger of the C.D. Howe Memorial Foundation and the Private Planning Association of Canada. It is a nonprofit, nonpolitical organization seeking to contribute nonpartisan research findings and commentary on Canadian economic policy issues.

The guiding principle of the Institute is to conduct its research and analysis in a manner that is balanced in approach, professional in method and readable in style.

To ensure diversity in perspective, participation is encouraged from organised labour, business, agricultural associations, and the professions.

While its focus is national, the Institute recognizes that Canada is composed of regions, each of which may have a particular point of view on policy issues, unique interests and concerns, and different concepts of national priorities. The Institute also pursues involvement from both of Canada's major linguistic communities.

It is not the purpose of the Institute to promote consensus on policy issues, although on occasion that may be feasible. The primary function is to add to public understanding of issues by providing sound analysis reflecting objective treatment of diverse points of view.

Although governments and their departments are excluded from Institute membership, the staff of the Institute seeks to develop good working relationships with public officials for the purpose of better understanding the basis for government decisions and contributing effectively to public policy formulation.

The immediate direction of the policies, program and staff of the Institute is vested in the Executive Director operating under the general direction of the President. The function of the Board of Directors, to whom the President is accountable, is to make independent research and publication possible under the most favourable conditions and not to control the conduct and conclusions of research activity.

Carl E. Beigie is President, Wendy Dobson is Executive Director and Treasurer, and Janet Hatfield is Corporate Secretary.

The Institute's publications are available at its offices, 2275 Bayview Avenue, Toronto, Ontario M4N 3M6 (Tel: 416-485-4310), Suite 2040, 1155 Metcalfe Street, Montreal, Quebec H3B 2X7 (Tel: 514-879-1254), and P.O. Box 1621, Calgary, Alberta T2P 2L7.

Publications of the British-North American Committee

BN-32 *Trade Issues in the Mid 1980s,* by Sidney Golt and a Committee Policy Statement, October 1982 (£3.50, $7.00)

BN-31 *The Newly Industrializing Countries: Adjusting to Success,* by Neil McMullen, October 1982 (£3.50, $7.00)

BN-30 *Conflicts of National Laws with International Business Activity: Issues of Extraterritoriality,* by A. H. Hermann, August 1982 (£3.00, $6.00)

BN-29 *Industrial Innovation in the United Kingdom, Canada and the United States,* by Kerry Schott, July 1981 (£2.25, $5.")

BN-28 *Flexible Exchange Rates and International Business,* by John M. Blin, Stuart I. Greenbaum and Donald J. Jacobs, December 1981 (£3.00, $8.00)

BN-27 *A Trade Union View of US Manpower Policy,* by William W. Winpisinger, April 1980 (£1.75, $3.00)

BN-26 *A Positive Approach to the International Economic Order, Part II: Non-Trade Issues,* by Alasdair MacBean and V. N. Balasubramanyam, May 1980 (£2.25, $5.00)

BN-25 *New Patterns of World Mineral Development,* by Raymond F. Mikesell, September 1979 (£2.25, $5.00)

BN-24 *Inflation is a Social Malady,* by Carl Beigie, March 1979 (£2.00, $4.00)

BN-23 *A Positive Approach to the International Economic Order, Part I: Trade & Structural Adjustment,* by Alasdair MacBean, October 1978 (£1.75, $3.00)

BN-22 *The GATT Negotiations 1973-79: The Closing Stage,* by Sidney Golt and a Committee Policy Statement, May 1978 (£1.50, $3.00)

BN-21 *Skilled Labour Supply Imbalances: The Canadian Experience,* by William Dodge, November 1977 (£1.50, $3.00)

BN-20 *The Soviet Impact on world Grain Trade,* by D. Gale Johnson, May 1977 (£1.75, $3.00)

BN-19 *Mineral Development in the Eighties: Prospects and Problems,* a Report Prepared by a Group of Committee Members with a Statistical Annex by Sperry Lea, November 1976 (£1.50, $3.00)

BN-18 *Skilled Labour Shortages in the United Kingdom: With Particular Reference to the Engineering Industry,* by Gerry Eastwood, October 1976 (£1.50, $3.00)

BN-17 *Higher Oil Prices: Worldwide Financial Implications,* a Policy Statement by the British-North American Committee and a Research Report by Sperry Lea, October 1975 (£1.50, $3.00)

BN-16 *Completing the GATT: Toward New International Rules to Govern Export Controls,* by C. Fred Bergsten, October 1974 (80p, $2.00)

BN-15 *Foreign Direct Investment in the United States: Opportunities and Impediments,* by Simon Webley, September 1974 (80p, $2.00)

BN-14 *The GATT Negotiations, 1973-75: A Guide to the Issues,* by Sidney Golt, April 1974 (£1.00, $2.50)

BN-13 *Problems of Economic Development in the Caribbean,* by David Powell, compiled from a study by Irene Hawkins, November 1973 (80p, $2.00)

BN-12 *The European Approach to Worker-Management Relationships,* by Innis Macbeth, October 1973 (£1.00, $2.50)

BN-11 *An International Grain Reserve Policy,* by Timothy Josling, July 1973 (40p, $1.00)

BN-10 *Man and His Environment,* by Harry G. Johnson, May 1973 (40p, $1.00)

OCCASIONAL PAPER-1 *New Investment in Basic Industries,* prepared by a Committee Task Force, June 1974 (60p, $1.00)

Publications of the British-North American Committee are available from:

In Great Britain and Europe	In the United States of America	In Canada
BRITISH-NORTH AMERICAN RESEARCH ASSOCIATION	NATIONAL PLANNING ASSOCIATION	C. D. HOWE INSTITUTE
1 Gough Square	1606 New Hampshire Avenue, NW	2275 Bayview Avenue
London EC4A 3DE	Washington	Toronto, Ontario
Tel. 01-353 6371	DC 20009	M4N 3M6
	Tel. 202 265 7685	Tel. 416 485 4310